A SYNOPSIS
OF THE BIBLE

(SECOND EDITION)

This book is written:

FOR THE NON-BELIEVER - Who is seeking knowledge

FOR THE NEW BELIEVER - Who is seeking understanding

FOR THE EXPERIENCED BELIEVER - Who is seeking coherence

WAYNE SHERMAN

authorHOUSE®

AuthorHouse™
1663 Liberty Drive
Bloomington, IN 47403
www.authorhouse.com
Phone: 1 (800) 839-8640

Published by AuthorHouse 03/03/2016

ISBN: 978-1-5049-8020-3 (sc)
ISBN: 978-1-5049-8021-0 (e)

Library of Congress Control Number: 2016902577

Print information available on the last page.

Any people depicted in stock imagery provided by Thinkstock are models, and such images are being used for illustrative purposes only. Certain stock imagery © Thinkstock.

This book is printed on acid-free paper.

ACKNOWLEDGEMENT

I started this document originally because of my stepdaughter, Sandy. Sandy is in her 40s, has been married and divorced twice and has three children, high school age and beyond. And she lives a thousand miles away. In a phone call a few months ago, Sandy confessed a belief in Jesus Christ as her personal savior. About a week later she asked her mother and I for a Bible and explained that she was dating an openly Christian young man, who was encouraging her to go to church with him. We sent her one. Then in a subsequent phone call she said she was having some trouble understanding the scriptures and how they all fit together. That is when I started this document. I sent her a partial draft a little later, and she thanked me for it. Since then I have sent her several updates. She let us know she was reading it and that it was making things clearer. I have not talked to her much recently about this document, but I hope it has helped her. Since then I have continued in this effort, because I thought it might be valuable to some others like Sandy, who may have lost their way in knowing and interpreting the messages of the Bible, and are struggling for a better understanding.

I have not sought out any particular source material for the following, except for the Bible itself and my personal memory and understanding from a lifetime of reading the Bible and listening to many teachers of the Word. If I have made some blunders, it is my own fault.

REASON FOR THIS UPDATE

This second edition is:

- to correct grammar and syntax errors in my original document,

- to add additional information that I felt would help readers to understand and properly interpret the Bible scriptures,

- to correct or clarify some of my interpretations of what the Bible said or meant

- and to add-in the Old Testament book of Ecclesiastes that I inadvertently left out of the original publication

Almost all the text and the intent of this document remain the same, including that of clarifying the background and purposes of the various parts of the Judeo/Christian Bible and the justification of its importance and relevance for individuals today and for modern society.

DISCLAIMER

This document, like my first edition, is in no way intended to replace or substitute for the reading of the Bible itself. This updated document again only touches the surface of the content and themes of the Bible. One may not find it inspirational, only informational. Real inspiration should primarily come from reading the Bible itself and delving into both the primary and secondary lessons which are often clear only when taken in context, or may be discerned with deeper study and understanding of its messages. However, great peace, inspiration, and answers to deep questions of faith and revelation can often come from reading only a few verses. There is power in the Bible that is not in this document. Please think of this document only as an introduction and guide for real Bible study.

FOREWORD

The Judeo/Christian Bible is a collection of the historical lore and writings of a number of different authors, documented over a period of about 2000 years. Most of the authors were descendants of a man, Abraham, who is considered the patriarch of the three most widespread of the world's religions; Jewish, Christian, and Muslim. All of these authors lived in the Middle East or Greece. The last of the writings were penned in about 90 AD. This collection of writings is recognized as the most complete, continuous record of the history of the Universe and the World from the beginning of time, until the end of the first century AD. The Bible, as we know it today, was an assembly of these writings in about 325 AD by a group of prominent and devoted Christian scholars, at the direction of Constantine, the emperor of the Roman Empire at that time. Their mission was not only to collect all pertinent writings, but also to sort through them to determine if authorship could be verified, and to determine which of the writings were really inspired by God. The language of this new Bible was then translated in about 385 AD into Vulgate, the language of the common people of the Roman Empire at the time by the Roman scholar Jerome, to allow reading and understanding by all. Since then it has gone through many translations and interpretations. A number of modern authors since have also published "Paraphrased" versions that have been attempts to either clarify the Bible text or to slant meanings to support various views of those authors. A huge number of books and publications have also been written in an effort to understand

and teach the in-depth meanings of various Bible passages. This document is none of these. It is intended, rather, to try to identify and emphasize the main themes and messages of the various books of the Bible and to show how they and their messages fit together theologically and historically. Some of the books appear to be most appropriate primarily for the time period in which they were written, but contain ideas that transcend those time periods. Others, contain messages and prophesies primarily for the times to come. I hope I have properly represented them all. Also, I hope that no more is read into this document, and I hope that I have not committed basic theological errors in my ideas of what the "main themes" are. Also, I have tried to avoid theological or "Christianese" idioms, so it is more easily understandable by non-churched readers. Hopefully, I have achieved these intents.

Various pastors, authors, and teachers extract individual passages or groups of passages from the Bible to help better understanding of the Bible and its messages, and to encourage commitment to the moral and ethical standards contained in it, and also to promote a belief in the Creator God (who is judgmental and all knowing, but also all caring); and for Christians, the acceptance of Jesus Christ as (1) the predicted fulfillment of the prophesies of the Old Testament, (2) a teacher offering a new way of living not bound to the "Jewish Law" of the Old Testament, and (3) the "Lamb (sacrifice) of God" who died that believers might have eternal life beyond the physical grave, fulfilling the predictions and prophesies in the Old Testament.

Many people are encouraged to read the Bible or to have a daily devotion that includes the reading of passages from the Bible. The intent of this is that Bible readers will be strengthened and heartened in their beliefs, will be given hope in difficult situations, will find peace within themselves, and will accept and commit to the faith that proposes an order to existence and a place, or state, of reward for the faithful. However, reading and receiving interpretations of individual Bible passages, though fulfilling, can often be confusing to the understanding of the message of the Bible as a whole. Some passages seem to contradict each other and others seem to not fit in with the rest of the document. Some passages seem quite brutal and others very loving and forgiving. I believe that it is important to see the picture and message of the Bible as a whole, in order, especially for the new initiates, to fully grasp the concepts the Bible contains. Thus, the following.

INTRODUCTION

The purpose of this document is not primarily to inspire the reader to be won over or to be more devoted, spiritual, or committed to one's faith, but rather to provide a framework and encouragement for more in-depth study of the Judeo/Christian Bible in order to possibly achieve those ends. It is structured in such a way to provide a synopsis of each of the individual books of the Bible, in order to indicate the major themes and messages of those books, and to show how they fit together, historically, theologically, and spiritually to provide a coherent flow of the stories and doctrines contained in it. Also in this document, I have attempted to indicate some of the tie-ins between the Bible and other historical events as well as modern concerns and issues. The reader may find more relevance than imagined. Thus, it is a must read for anyone who may be intimidated or confused by what they are finding in attempts at Bible study.

First of all, the Bible is separated in two major sections, the old and the new testaments. The **Old Testament** begins with the history of the creation of the universe, and then continues with, more specifically, the establishment of the Jewish nation and its being set apart by God, the creator of that universe. It is also the story of the growth and survival of that nation through about 1500 years from its establishment to the advent of the New Testament. The **New Testament** is the story of the life, teachings, and purposes of Jesus, the Christ prophesied in the Old

Testament, and which provides a concrete basis the fulfillment of those prophesies.

Except for the first five books of the Old Testament (called the TORAH), the various books of the Old Testament were not originally part of one document. The other Old Testament books, which were written by various authors over the period of time after the TORAH, were added beginning in about the second century BC by Jewish scholars. At that time those scholars rejected several books called as a group "The Apocrypha" which were deemed not inspired by God, or which did not contribute to the purpose of the Bible. The New Testament books were added to the Old Testament in the third century AD by a group of Christian priests and scholars under the direction of Roman Emperor Constantine. Again, several books were rejected as not inspired by God. *(Note that some of the books of the Apocrypha, such as the book of Tobit, have been resurrected by the Catholic Church and are now part of the official Bible of the Catholic Church. However, most of the evangelical Christian churches use and accept the Bible translations that include only the books as set forth in version authorized in the third century AD. This document includes summaries of only those books.)* All the books were probably originally written in the Hebrew or Aramaic language, although they were translated early on into Greek and later into Latin. As indicated in the "Forward" above, the first complete Bible was translated into the Latin language, (the common language of the time, so most people could read and understand it). At first, the books of the Bible were not divided into chapters and verses. These divisions were added later to help people to study and further understand the messages contained in it.

A SYNOPSIS OF THE OLD TESTAMENT

T hough the Old Testament covers the history of the universe from its creation to about 300 years before the coming of Jesus Christ, it is primarily about the creation, history, and struggles of a people set aside by God to represent him on earth. It includes the designation of one couple, Abraham and Sarah, to be the progenitors of that people group and the subsequent journey of that people group to Egypt, which lead to their enslavement, their liberation, and their return to the land area originally given to Abraham, as well as the establishment of their culture as a nation. It then tells of growth and turmoil of that nation as it progresses to the establishment of a regional empire, the splitting of that empire, the deportation of its people, and the reestablishment of a nation state by a small remnant of that people group, with its capital at Jerusalem. It also contains key prophesies as to the coming of Christ.

The books of about the first half of the Old Testament are books of history of the world and of the nation that grew from the descendants of the man, Abraham. Also they provide the laws that set the standards for conduct and worship of a society and culture for those descendants. These books of history are then followed by a collection of stories, songs and sayings of people who believed in God and tried to understand and act on his will and plan. The third section of the Old Testament contains the writings those who are considered "major prophets".

These books provide some historical data, but also contain a significant portion of the Biblical prophesies about future national and world events. The books of fourth section of the Old Testament are called the "minor prophets". They also contain many prophesies. The only real reason that they are distinguished from the third section is that these books are shorter. All four sections are described below with one or more paragraphs about each book.

The History Books

The first Book of the Bible is **GENESIS**. This is basically a book of history. But it also contains significant guidance from God to early people in human history. It starts with the beginning of all things, the universe, and the world. It then jumps to the creation of man. A lot of the well known people and stories of the Bible are mentioned in this book; Adam and Eve (the first creatures made in God's image) and their fall from grace, Cain and Abel (a story of the definition of acceptable vs. unacceptable sacrifices and of jealousy between brothers), and the great flood (including the story of Noah and the Ark). The flood saga identifies Noah and his three sons and their wives as the only human survivors of the flood. One of the sons was named Shem and another one was named Ham, thus creating a division in human culture that survives to this day. (The descendants of Shem (Semites) have been identified with the modern day Jews and the descendants of Ham as other modern day Middle Eastern people.) Genesis also tells of the building of the Tower of Babel (where the nations were driven apart because they tried to challenge the power of God. The way God drove them apart was to cause them to loose the ability to speak a common language). It also contains the calling of Abraham and Sarah (Semites) to move from what is now southern Iraq, to an area now part of northwestern Iraq, and then later to the area of the world now called Israel (a semi-mountainous area between the Jordan River and the east end of the Mediterranean Sea), and also there to be the progenitors of the Jewish nation. Accompanying Abraham was Lot, Abraham's nephew. In addition, it contains records of the first known war (between kings [tribal leaders] from the area that is now Iraq and the city states that then existed in Israel). It also details the destruction of Sodom and Gomorrah. (The Bible is specific in the reason that Sodom and Gomorrah were destroyed because the male citizens there demanded to have homosexual sex with both men and angels.) It also records the ascension of the one of the great grandchildren of Abraham (Joseph) to be the prime minister of Egypt, and the migration of Abraham's descendents (by that time a tribe of about 70 people) to Egypt. Genesis ends about in 2000 BC. Several of the events in Genesis also appear in other history records of ancient Iraq, Iran, and Egypt.

The next book, **EXODUS**, jumps ahead to a period beginning about 300 plus years later. It starts with the birth and maturing of Moses (a descendant of Abraham) in Egypt, and his call by God to lead his fellow descendants of Abraham back out of Egypt to the territory where Abraham and his descendants had lived before they moved to Egypt. By the time of Moses, Abraham's descendents had become slaves of the Egyptians, and apparently had been involved in building several of the great cities and temples of old Egypt. They, also by this time, had become known as "Hebrews". Moses was a Hebrew but was raised as an Egyptian in the court of the king (Pharaoh). As an adult he learned his true heritage and determined to rescue his people from slavery. This book includes the stories of ten plagues that befell the Egyptians that forced them to eventually allow the Hebrews to leave Egypt. This saga includes the establishment of the **Passover** (to protect the Hebrew people from being killed by the last of these plagues). It also tells of the crossing of the Red Sea by the Hebrews to escape from Egypt after the pharaoh changed his mind. The **Ten Commandments** first appear in this book. It also includes actions by Moses to set up a new religion and government for this new Hebrew nation. He also created, under God's direction, a design for a "tabernacle" (a large, portable tent, to act as a central place of worship) for the new nation. In addition he documented a set of rules, "Laws" for the Hebrew people to live by.

The third book of the Bible, **LEVITICUS**, is a whole book of additional rules for worship and living, recorded by Moses. It also sets up a hierarchy of ruling authority for the people. A number of these rules involve the killing and sacrificing of animals, which were an important part of the original Hebrew religion.

The theme of the fourth book, **NUMBERS**, is primarily a record of two censuses conducted by Moses to determine the size and makeup of the new nation. The population consisted of the 12 tribes of Israel, each the descendents of one of the sons of Jacob, the grandson of Abraham. It specifically sets up the tribe of Levi as the servants of worship (deacons and church administrators) and the descendents of Moses' brother Aaron as the family of priests (pastors). It also contains some additional rules for living, and records the beginning of wars of conquest to retake the land of Israel, which had been left to other people when Abraham's descendents migrated to Egypt 400 years earlier.

The fifth book, **DEUTERONOMY**, is basically a reiteration the previous three books (Exodus, Leviticus, and Numbers). As such, it restates the Ten Commandments and a lot of the other laws and rules for worship and living (including the roles of men and women in a marriage) that are contained in those previous books. It particularly emphasizes that the primary commandment is to "Love the Lord with all your heart, soul and mind". This is the first law of God quoted by Jesus in the New Testament. It also very strongly promotes the teaching of children to remember that God is the only real God so that the faith in Him is perpetuated from generation to generation. In addition it also reiterates the miracles that created the Hebrew nation. It appears to be made of three parts, two speeches of instructions by Moses to the Hebrews, and the third, a record of the death of Moses and the appointment of his successor, Joshua. In this book, Moses predicted future exile events to befall the Hebrew people **and the coming of a Christ** (a final and all powerful ruler).

The books Exodus through Deuteronomy record a period of time of about 120 years corresponding to the life of Moses. **With the book of Genesis added, these books are considered the core of the Jewish Bible. Together, these books are considered by some Jewish people today as the only real Bible.**

Next, the book of **JOSHUA** is another history book. It records several very bloody events in the conquest of the land of Israel under the leadership of Joshua. It contains the story of the fall of the walls of Jericho and annihilation of whole cities, including men, women and children at the hands of the Hebrew people. It also includes several examples of the failure of the Hebrews in their attempts at conquest when they didn't follow God's leadership. In addition, it contains assignment of the conquered lands to 11 of the 12 tribes to set up their homes and properties, and to build their cities. (The tribe of Levi was not separately assigned land but rather to be responsible for worship. Instead the other tribes were asked to volunteer land from their assignments for use by the Levites). An interesting item is the setting up of "cites of refuge" where people guilty of committing wrongs toward others could escape to avoid revenge. The last part of the book records a general degradation of the will of the people to carry out the annihilation of the sinful people who inhabited Israel before the Hebrews arrived, thus leaving incomplete God's mission of conquest by the Hebrews. It concludes with the death of Joshua.

Then, the book of **JUDGES**, another history book, tells of a period of time after Joshua, about 400 years, when Israel was basically leaderless, except for a series of "Judges" who were responsible for adjudicating disputes brought by individuals against other individuals, and for sometimes acting individually or as leaders to repulse foreign invaders. The first part of the book details the failure of the Hebrews to carry out God's command to rid the area of the other people groups who lived there, and the consequences of their failure to do so. The tabernacle (central tent of worship created by Moses) was set up in the new land conquered by the Hebrews, probably in or near the little town of Bethel, about the middle of the captured territory, and was cared for by the Levites and the descendents of Aaron. When the people had a dispute between each other, they came to the tabernacle to obtain a judgment. Several of the judges and their exploits as military leaders are documented in Judges.

A number of people of neighboring nations came in as raiding parties and stole the possessions of the Hebrew people and enslaved some of them. Some of the exploits of the judges were to drive out the invaders and obtain the release of the captured people. One of the stories in this book is about the first woman judge, Deborah and the leader of her army, Barak, who won a war against the one of these invaders. Another notable person in this book is Samson and how he was destroyed by his impetuous nature and by an unfaithful wife. It also contains the story of Gideon, who, with God's help, organized a small band of soldiers to drive out a much larger army of raiders. This is the Gideon that has become the name of the group that now places Gideon Bibles in hotel rooms. Unfortunately, it also records the eventual corruption of Gideon by riches and power.

The next book is the story of **Ruth**. Ruth was a Moabite girl (the Moabites were descended from Lot, Abraham's nephew and who were sometimes enemies of the Hebrews) who was engaged to a boy who was the son of a Hebrew woman, Naomi. Naomi had moved to the country of Moab with her husband. Unfortunately, both Naomi's husband and her son, Ruth's fiancé, died. So Naomi decided to move back to Israel. Ruth loved the mother of her dead fiancé and decided to go with her and to accept her God. Back in Israel, Ruth met and married an Israelite landowner, and became the grandmother of David, a future king of Israel. It is short book, a very romantic story, and well worth reading. It also, seems to have a message that it was OK for Hebrew people to marry outside their people group, but only if it is part of God's plan.

By about 1100 BC, the priests and Levites had become corrupt, and the people of Israel became tired being walked on by surrounding nations, so they decided they wanted a king to unify and rule the nation, and to raise an army to defend it against other nations. The books of **1ˢᵗ and 2ⁿᵈ SAMUEL** tell of the end of the era of the Judges and the establishment of the kingdom of Israel. The book of **1ˢᵗ CHRONICLES,** besides going back to the beginning of time and the universe, also summarizes this same period. The people of Israel picked their own first king, Saul, who was young, tall, strong, and hansom, with a kingly air about him. He was from the tribe of Benjamin. He built an army and protected the people, but unfortunately, he had serious character flaws. One was he did not properly respect God or his mentor, the judge Samuel, and took the process of worship into his own hands. He also became by-polar and had fits of rage. So God sent out Samuel to pick another King to replace Saul. He picked, with God's guidance, David, of the tribe of Judah. David wasn't tall and kingly looking like Saul, but he was good looking and had an intensity about him that drew people to him. He first came into prominence by joining Saul's army and killing a giant, Goliath, a huge warrior in the army of the Philistines, enemies of the Hebrews. (An aside, the Philistines lived in an area now called the Gaza Strip.) After this, the people began to honor and praise David more than Saul, and Saul became jealous and set out to kill David. He tried but failed, and David actually became a musician in Saul's court, to sing and play music to calm Saul down when he flew into one of his rages. Then, Saul was killed by one of the armies he was fighting, and David became king, and became a much better leader than Saul. He captured the citadel of Jerusalem, moved the Tabernacle to there, and determined to build a permanent stone and wood temple in Jerusalem to replace the Tabernacle tent. David also wrote over half of the songs in the book of **Psalms**. Unfortunately, David, even though he was favored by God, also had moral and ethical problems. He stole his first wife from a wealthy land owner. When he became king, he married several more women and fathered numerous children by these different wives. And then a most memorable story about David is that he stole Bathsheba from her husband, a soldier in his army, and sent her husband into battle to be killed. This of course came back to haunt him. First, David made Bathsheba pregnant, and she had a child who died. Her second child by David was Solomon, who was his favorite. But David had several older sons by other wives, who were jealous of Solomon, so they rebelled and drove David out of Jerusalem. Those other sons were eventually killed, and David was restored to his throne, but to his great loss.

1ˢᵗ **KINGS** tells of the end of David's reign and the ascension of Solomon. The beginning of Solomon's reign was bloody, as he had to fight off and kill other contenders to the throne, from both David's and Saul's families and their followers. However, he became a good and wise king, noted for his very insightful judgments and decisions, and his leadership. He built the temple in Jerusalem that was conceived and designed by his father David, and expanded his kingdom to include part of modern day Egypt, all of modern day Lebanon, Jordan and Syria, and to the borders of modern day Turkey and Iraq. One of the interesting stories about Solomon was the visit of the queen of Sheba. Sheba was a country believed to be either modern day Yemen or Ethiopia. After Solomon died, the kingdom of Israel was split in two. The southern part, the territory of the descendents of the tribes of Benjamin, Judah, and remnants of the tribe of Simeon, took the name, Judah. It was to be ruled by a very nasty and corrupt son of Solomon named Rehoboam. This group of tribes was henceforth called the Southern Kingdom and the people who lived there became known as Jews. The other part, consisting of all the other tribes, split off under the kingship of Jeroboam, the prime minister under Solomon. He set up his capitol in Samaria in the territory of the tribe of Ephraim, about 50 miles north of Jerusalem. This group of tribes contained the majority of the Hebrew people, and who for the most part, were more affluent than those of the southern kingdom. They assumed the name Israel, and were sometimes called the Northern Kingdom. In order to fully separate Israel from Judah, Jeroboam set up high places of worship for the people of his kingdom, including one at Bethel, so that they would not return Jerusalem to worship in Solomon's temple.

During the rest of the history recorded in **1ˢᵗ KINGS, 2ⁿᵈ KINGS, and 1ˢᵗ and 2ⁿᵈ CHRONICLES**, everything went steadily down hill. Though there were a few good successor kings along the way, there were also some really bad ones who brought in high taxes, and forced labor, and who built temples and worship places to other gods, some involving male prostitutes and even the burning of small children alive. The northern kingdom went down hill faster. One thing that happened was that Jeroboam, the northern king repudiated God and started his own religion. **The people forgot their heritage and their loyalty to the God of Abraham and Moses, and became prosperous and complacent, (sounds familiar).** Later northern kings brought in the religions of neighboring countries by marrying princesses from those kingdoms who brought in their own gods, hence the story of Ahab and his wife, Jezebel. King Ahab wanted a piece of land that belonged to a prosperous farmer in the area. So, at Jezebel's urging, Ahab had the farmer killed and took the land. The prophet Elijah preached against him and condemned him for it, so Ahab tried to have him killed also. However, Ahab and Jezebel both met bad ends. Ahab was killed in a palace coup and Jezebel was thrown from a palace tower and eaten by wild dogs. Shortly thereafter, Sennacherib became king over an area now part of northern Iraq and northern Iran, then called Assyria. He conquered the northern kingdom and carried the country's treasures and a significant part of the population back to Assyria, where they disappeared from history. It is assumed that there they lost all commitment to their heritage, and intermarried with the Assyrian people. (They may have become ancestors of the Kurdish and other northern Iraqi people.) Thus, they became known as the lost tribes of Israel. Sennacherib then imported some lower class people from Assyria to repopulate the territory of Israel. The Israeli people who were not deported to Assyria intermarried with them, and their descendants later became known as "Samaritans". (See references to the Samaritans in the New Testament.) The southern kingdom lasted longer but didn't fare any better. About 100 years after the northern kingdom fell, Nebuchadnezzar, king over the city and nation of Babylon, a territory that is now southern Iraq and southern Iran, conquered them, and destroyed the temple in Jerusalem. His army took most of the citizens of Judah into captivity, to settle in and around Babylon in southern Iraq. This whole history of the Kings of Israel and Judah took about 450 years (the rise and fall of a prosperous nation).

About 70 years transpired between the end of the kingdom of Judah and the book of **EZRA**. During that time period, Nebuchadnezzar died. His kingdom was taken over by his grandson, Belshazzar. Shortly afterwards, his kingdom was conquered by the Medes and the Persians, (from modern northern Iran). One of the first things that the new king of Persia (Cyrus) did was let a group, about 70,000, of the people of Judah go back to Jerusalem and to rebuild the temple. **The descendents of these 70,000, and some other Jewish people who had not been deported from Judah to Iraq (who were apparently not important enough to be taken into captivity) are who continue to this day to be known as Jews.** A priest, Ezra, went with them. He tried to start a revival among the returnees, to stop intermarriage with non-Jews, and to rebuild the temple. But he ran into all sorts of problems with the Samaritans and other people who lived there by then, who stirred up trouble for him. So, much of the work of rebuilding Jerusalem and the temple were stopped.

About 90 years later, Cyrus had died and had been succeeded by Darius (Historical Note not in the Bible, Darius was the Persian king who tried to invade Greece but was defeated at Marathon). Darius was then succeeded by Xerxes (Historical Note not in the Bible: Xerxes also tried to invade Greece but was defeated at Thermopylae). Xerxes was succeeded to the Persian throne by his son Artaxerxes. The book of **NEHEMIAH** is the story of Nehemiah, a Jew, who's family didn't go back to Jerusalem with Ezra. However, he had heard about the problems that Ezra had had. He was a member of the court of Artaxerxes, so had some influence. So he asked and received permission from Artaxerxes to allow him to go to Jerusalem and to complete the rebuilding of the temple and the city walls as well. He was successful in both, as recorded in the book of Nehemiah. This book ends about 300 years before the birth of Christ and is the last book of the history of Judah/Israel in the Old Testament.

Historically, the next 200 or 300 years was a time of great turmoil for the Jewish people, and nothing of the history of the Jewish people during this period is recorded in the Constantine authorized Bible. However, as recorded in other historical accounts, the first item of significance was that Alexander the Great came to power in Greece and conquered all of the Persian Empire, including the part where Jerusalem was located. By this time, that area had become known as Judea. Alexander died at an early age and his kingdom was divided into four parts, each part ruled by a corrupt new pseudo-Greek king. The person who took over the area where Judea and Jerusalem were located, hated the Jews. So he and his descendants, the Selucids, did all sorts of things to desecrate their sacred places, including killing a number of the priests and slaughtering a pig on the sacred temple alter. There was a revolt under the Maccabees, a family of rebel leaders who were hailed for bringing freedom back to Judea. When the Maccabees liberated Judea, the people created the celebration of Hanukkah (the festival of Lights) to commemorate this event. However, the descendants of the Maccabees became corrupt and fell out of favor, and the Roman Empire absorbed Judea. With permission and protection of Rome and its army, Herod the Great then assumed the kingship of Judea, and was king of Judea at the time of the birth of Christ. Under his leadership, Nehemiah's temple was torn down, and a bigger, more pretentious building was built in its place. He also built several palaces and the fortress called Masada (which later figured in the destruction of Judea as a nation). During this period, Jewish scholars created a new document called the "Talmud", which greatly amplified, updated, and clarified the original laws of Moses.

Books of poetry, songs, philosophy, and guides for living

They are as follows:

King Ahasuerus, apparently another name for Xerxes, came to power in Persia when there were still Hebrew exiles living there. **ESTHER**, who was one of the Hebrew women still living in Persia, was selected to be one of Ahasuerus's (Xerxes's) wives. Esther had an uncle, Mordecai, who discovered a plot to kill all the Hebrews still living in Persia. The book of Esther tells of the plot and how it was foiled by the bravery of Esther. Interestingly, the way the Jews were saved was not to eliminate the people trying to kill them, although the chief instigator was executed, **but was instead to arm the Jews to defend themselves.** I think the message of this book is that God will take care of those who honor their families and heritage, and trust in Him for protection.

JOB, pronounced "Jobe", may be the oldest written book in the Bible. It is the story of a man who had everything; health, power, love, riches, friends, and family, but lost it all. However, through it all, he never lost his faith in God. His wife even suggested he give up and die. His friends came to visit and gave him all sorts of advice, including to admit that he did something wrong to deserve what happened to him. He swore that he was as blameless as any of his friends who were more successful, and asked God to tell him why these calamities had happed to him. Then God told him that he was not wise enough to intellectually understand. Instead of trying to understand, God told Job that he only needed to accept that

11

God is the all powerful and everlasting lord of the universe, and Job must believe in him unconditionally. When Job did, all was restored to him. This is a very powerful story and has real meaning for all humanity.

PSALMS is a book of songs, about half of which were written by King David, the best known of which is most likely the 23rd psalm. Some of David's songs were written when David had realized what terrible mistakes he had made in his life and was pleading for God's forgiveness. The rest were written by priests and believers during the time of the kingdoms described in Samuel, Kings and Chronicles. Many were used and sung during worship services. A few even show up in Handel's Messiah. Some actually predict the coming of a "Messiah". Many are quite emotional.

PROVERBS is a book of wise sayings and admonitions attributed to Solomon. It recommends a moral life style, and specifically talks about how to educate children to be moral, ethical, and responsible. The last chapter is particularly interesting in that it describes what a woman should be like as an ideal wife.

ECCLESIASTES is a book of the Bible written by King Solomon as he was nearing the end of his life. For some reason it appears in the Bible before the SONG OF SOLOMON even though that book was written by Solomon when he was younger. In Ecclesiastes, Solomon voiced his recognition that, even though he had achieved great riches, fame, and power as king of Israel, these things only fed his vanity, folly, and self indulgence, and that they really meant nothing in the circle of life. He said it was good to be wise, but wisdom does not save one from death. The third chapter begins with a quite well-known poem that says that there is a time for everything. As Solomon neared death, he began to realize that a belief and fear of God was more important than anything he had attained, that a good name is also important, and that often, patience and sorrow are better than success and happiness. He also reiterated the lesson of Job that we, as humans, cannot fully understand God's ways. The book ends with several admonitions. One is to respect authority, even though error and folly can be there as anywhere else in the world. Also, one should appreciate and enjoy the good things that God has provided, and recognize that often good things come even from bad situations.

Another admonition is to always recognize even when you are young that God is with you always, and that one should fear him and keep his commandments in good times and bad throughout one's life.

<u>SONG OF SOLOMON</u> is a love poem written as a duet between king Solomon and his lover as they declared their desperate love for each other, and as they prepared for and consummated their marriage. It is quite sexual in its words and innuendoes. Interestingly, tradition says that orthodox Jews were not allowed to read it until they were thirty years old. Its intensity is suggestive of the strength of the love we should have for God and that God has for us.

The major Old Testament Prophets

The first such book contains the prophesies of the prophet <u>ISAIAH</u>. This book was written by Isaiah and his scribe (stenographer). It was composed about the time after the split when both the northern and southern kingdoms were being threatened to be overrun by Sennacherib, the king of Assyria. Isaiah let people know in no uncertain terms that if they did not turn from their ways, they would be killed, starved, raped, or carried away into captivity; things that did later happen. However, people chose not to believe him. **Isaiah is best known for his prophesies about the coming of Christ, describing in detail that he would be born of a virgin, and what kind of person Christ would be and how he would be treated (badly).** Several of his writings are included as songs in Handel's Messiah. The period of time in which Isaiah wrote his prophesies included the period of the conquest of Israel by the Assyrian king, Sennacherib and the beginning of the rise to power of the city kingdom of Babylon under king Nebuchadnezzar in what is now southern Iraq and Iran. Tradition (not in the Bible) says that his enemies put Isaiah to death by placing him inside a hollow log and sawing him in half.

<u>JEREMIAH</u> is also a major prophet. This book is written by Jeremiah, a prophet just before and during the time of the final destruction of Judah and Jerusalem by Nebuchadnezzar. His message was basically the same

as of Isaiah some years before. The leaders of Judah again did not want to listen. He prophesied that both Israel and Judah would eventually be restored. For his prophesies, he was put in a muddy cistern to starve to death. However, some of his believing followers got him out and saved his life. He suffered through the destruction of Jerusalem and was eye witness to the chaos and barbarity of those left behind, who fought against each other for power and dominance among the refugees (somewhat like "Mad Max" or other apocalypse movie scenarios). According to tradition, Jeremiah eventually escaped with some of his followers to Egypt, where apparently he died. He also, like Isaiah, predicted the coming of Christ.

LAMENTATIONS is a book of poems written by Jeremiah, lamenting the sad state of man, and his fall as a result of his weaknesses. It contains some well known passages and is quite worth reading for its truth and wisdom.

EZEKIEL, also a major prophet, was carried away to southern Iraq during the last deportation (by Nebuchadnezzar). In his prophesies, he tried to convince the people who were deported with him to stick with God so they could return to their homeland. He did some weird and picturesque things to get his message over, including starving himself, making and building strange things, and refusing to speak, using only sign language. He described visions he had that sounded strangely like science fiction, and E.T.s, and strange vehicles from outer space. One of his most well know prophesies had to do with a valley of dry bones (a prediction of bringing back to life of the nation of Judah). He was fearful that the people wouldn't listen to his message. God told him that this was all right, that as long as he tried his best, their souls would not be on his head.

DANIEL was one of several very intelligent and driven teenagers in the court of the king of Judah when Nebuchadnezzar's army destroyed Jerusalem. They were deported to Babylon and chosen to be trained for service in Nebuchadnezzar's court. In the first part of the book of Daniel, he wrote about his commitment to his people and the Jewish law, and the miraculous rescue of his three friends, Shadrach, Meshach, and Abednego, from being burned alive in a furnace. They had been condemned to die there for sticking to their Jewish faith. Daniel also was able to interpret dreams, and was honored by Nebuchadnezzar for this. Nebuchadnezzar subsequently made Daniel his chief advisor. The book also recounts how Nebuchadnezzar went insane and lived like an animal for seven years until he learned to respect God. Daniel lived a long life, probably due to his healthy life style, and was still alive when that Medes and Persians from northern Iran conquered the Babylonian empire. He then became an advisor to Cyrus and then Darius, Persian kings. He prophesied the rise and fall of the several successive empires, Persian, Greek, pseudo-Greek, and Roman and also the coming of Christ, as well as prophesies about the end of times. However, he got in trouble with Cyrus, who threw him into a den of lions. Cyrus was surprised and actually pleased when Daniel immerged from the lion's den the next day, unscathed.

Minor Old Testament Prophets

After Daniel is a section of the Old Testament that contains the writings of those who were called the "minor prophets".

The first of these is **HOSEA**. It is a story of how Hosea's wife left him and their children, and became a prostitute. Hosea found her and took her back. It is an allegory of how the people of Israel turned away from God, and God's effort to first point out their crimes and then try to bring them back into His family and His good graces. However, Hosea predicts that Israel will refuse God's mercy and turn away from Him and will fall by the sword

The next minor prophet is **JOEL**. He predicted the invasion of Sennacherib, and compared his army to a swarm of killer locust to bring judgment and justice to Israel.

Next, **AMOS** was a sheep herder in Judah, but he went to the northern kingdom with strong prophesies about the destruction of Israel and other nations around it. His method of writing is quite unique and powerful, in that he used the phrase over and over "for three transgressions and for four".

Next, **OBADIAH** predicted the destruction of the nation of Edom, a neighbor of Judah. Interestingly, Edom was the home of the descendents of Abraham but not of the lineage of the Jews (The Edomites were descendants Jacob's disinherited twin brother, Esau, a grandson of Abraham). Also, Herod the Great, king of Judea when Jesus was born, was apparently part Edomite.

Next, **JONAH** is probably the most interesting of the minor prophets. He was called by God to be a missionary to Assyria, the kingdom which a couple of hundred years later was led by King Sennacherib, who invaded and destroyed the northern kingdom. Jonah hated the Assyrians and did not want to preach to them. So he booked passage on a ship to Cyprus, an island in the Mediterranean Sea. The ship met with a violent storm, and the crew decided it was Jonah's fault. They threw him into the sea. And a fish, specially prepared by God, swallowed him. Three days later, the fish vomited Jonah up on shore, alive. So he decided to go to Assyria and preach after all. He did so and made a lot of converts to belief in God. But, he was still angry, so he built for himself a vine-covered arbor overlooking Nineveh, Assyria's capitol, to live in, to watch and hope for the destruction of the city. It didn't happen, but insects attacked Jonah's arbor and killed the vine that was his shade. So he gave up and went home. He had many problems because he had a mission but didn't trust God's direction to carry it out. Aside: as indicated above, the conversion of the Assyrians to belief in God didn't prevent them from later invading and destroying Israel (See Nahum below).

MICAH was a contemporary of Isaiah. He condemned the rich and powerful for mistreating the poor. **He also predicted the coming of Christ and that Christ would be born in Bethlehem.** This was about 700 years before Christ was born.

NAHUM predicted the destruction of Israel by Assyria, who, a couple of hundred years after Jonah had led many conversions there, had apparently forgotten what Jonah had taught them.

HABAKKUK prophesied during the hundred years or so between the invasions of Israel and Judah by Assyria under Sennacherib and by

Babylon under Nebuchadnezzar. He stated that sometimes God might use a wicked nation to do his will, but indicated that **"the righteous shall live by faith"**, a later message of the New Testament.

ZEPHANIAH pronounced God's judgment on the wicked, both inside and outside Israel and Judah, and predicted the end of time.

HAGGAI and ZECHARIAH lived in Jerusalem after the return of the 70,000 from Babylon during the time of Ezra. They helped encourage the people to rebuild the temple as a symbol of God's presence among them and again as a center for worship.

MALACHI is the last book of the Old Testament (but not necessarily the last one written. (That was probably Nehemiah). Malachi encouraged the people of Judea to support God's work with a 'Tithe" (Giving a tenth of one's income to the benefit of God). **He also predicted the coming of both John the Baptist and Jesus Christ.**

Old Testament General Summary

In summary: The Old Testament spans a historic period from the beginning of time, to about 300 years before the beginning of the ministry of Jesus Christ. It is unique in that it is the most consistent and unbroken written record of history of the pre-Christian era, better than anything created by any other civilization of the period. But, its focus is not on history so much as on the selection, establishment, and the training by God the creator, of a chosen people, the Hebrews, to be a blessing to all of civilization. As we can see, this took a while, with many fits and starts. God had to make man realize the nuances of successful human existence and civilized living. Abraham is recognized as the first person set aside for this special assignment. But many of his descendents were lost to the historical record, and only a relatively small group (the Jewish people) exists today within the 7,000,000,000 persons who now populate the world.

But, in order to validate one of the two main successes of God's plan, we must recognize, despite the fact that those who have maintained the Jewish heritage, even though a relatively quite small group within the world's population today, they have been protected by God as a blessing on all of humanity. To support this thesis, as a group, they now control a significant portion of the world banking systems, hold a remarkable number of the world's patents, have won an exceptional number of Nobel Prizes, play a major role in the creation and performance of the art and music known today, and have a large role today in both the technology and the entertainment industries.

The other, and <u>biggest</u>, success is "Christianity", which provides the basis for civilization and civilized governments in an otherwise chaotic world. More on this later.

Old Testament Themes.

There are several recurring themes in the Old Testament.

<u>The first theme is that God, was the creator of the Universe</u>, and as such is all knowledgeable, all powerful and all seeing, and is the only real God, and that he <u>created man</u> to worship and fear (have respect and reverence for) him.

<u>A second theme is the establishment of absolute rights and wrongs and for laws to live by.</u> The predominant basis for these laws is the Ten Commandments, provided to Moses by God himself. They cover the gamut of how to live in this world as honorable human beings and to work together to establish and maintain a purpose for life and for the perpetuation of civilized society. Without them, I believe that there would be no coherent civilization.

There is however an interesting paradox in those original Ten Commandments in that the commandments which refer to civil society, and are more well-known and more integrated into our legal systems, are not the first ones stated in the commandment list. Everybody knows about commandments 6 through 10; (6) don't commit murder, (7) don't have illicit sex, (8) don't steal, (9) don't lie when it can hurt somebody, (10) don't crave anything that belongs to someone else and try to take it away from them. **Most <u>civil</u> laws are based on these last five.**

Also a lot of civilizations try to follow the fifth commandment, "have respect for your parents", even to the point of sometimes building a whole religion around this one (ancestor worship). This also extends to remembering one's heritage and being able build on that heritage to further the growth of social order.

But the commandments that most people seem to most frequently ignore, are what are considered in the Bible to be the most important. These are the first four. They are: (1) You shall worship the creator God, and him only. (2) You shall not make images of anything for the purpose of worshiping those images, or worship any images even made by others, or natural wonders, instead of God himself. (I think this includes statues of saints or even magnificent church buildings, or images of sex, power and prestige.) (Interestingly, this particular commandment includes a threat of punishment for not only the breakers of this commandment, but also on several generations of descendants.) (3) Don't use the Lord's name in vain, but respect it (simply, don't swear maliciously, or even as a casual emphasis to speech, or in frustration). (4) Remember to always set aside a special day (the Sabbath) out of every seven to relax and to worship God. These first four commandments, though considered most important in the Bible, are, as I said above, often unfortunately ignored by most people.

<u>A third theme is that there needs to be a sacrifice to atone for wrong doing</u>. A significant part of the Torah is the instructions on how and when to offer sacrifices, many of which are blood sacrifices. This means that the wrongdoer must give up a part of his possessions or well-being or in order to be forgiven. There are several examples where people brought on themselves the sacrifice of their own lives by their own wrongdoing. But, the Bible provides examples of when a man of faith would try to offer as a sacrifice another human life, God always gave him a substitute (i.e. when Abraham tried to sacrifice his son Isaac, see below). This also is a premonition of the "Passover" in the Book of Exodus and later the sacrifice of Christ on the cross in the New Testament.

A fourth theme is the "blood" sacrifice. God wanted the killing of some living being as a sacrifice as proof of respect for him. Adam's son, Abel's, blood sacrifice was acceptable to God, but Cain's grain sacrifice was not. When Noah got off the arc he offered a blood sacrifice as thanks to God for his survival. Abraham offered blood sacrifices for worship and victories in battle. Abraham also offered his only son, Isaac, as a blood sacrifice. But significantly, God didn't let him do it. Instead God gave him an animal substitute. Moses instructed the people of Israel, still captive in Egypt, to sacrifice a lamb for the first "Passover" to protect them from a killing plague. Then, after their release from Egypt, he built a whole set of rules around blood sacrifices for people to use to ask for forgiveness. These sacrifice rules were used throughout the pre-Christian era, and were adopted by other societies as well. Also, one of the rules of such sacrifice was that it was to be the best member of one's flock or possessions, and not a cull or sick animal.

A fifth theme was the way God treated his chosen people. He treated them like a parent would, to help children grow and learn right from wrong, rewarding them for doing right, and sometimes severely punishing them for doing wrong. He even let bullying, non-believing rulers of other nations to come in and devastate his own people in order to teach them lessons. One of the main lessons was to stay the course, and don't forget God, even in the midst of hardship and peer pressure, but especially in times of prosperity when people felt they could depend on themselves rather than God.

A sixth theme was that when God granted men permission to do something, men tried to do it their way and not God's, and thereby failed to do it right. For example: Cain offered a grain sacrifice to God instead of a blood sacrifice. He ended up killing his brother Abel and being driven off into oblivion. Abraham decided to have a child by his wife's servant instead of his wife. He had a child, Ishmael, who's descendants are recognized as the mostly Muslim Arabs, enemies of Israel today. When the Israelites were led out of Egypt by Moses, they tried to set up their own religion instead of the one that God ordained, and many died as a result. God let the people of Israel have a king, but they made their own choice, not God's. So they ended up with Saul, a manic depressive who had to be replaced by God's choice, David. The northern kingdom spit off from worship of God to follow other religions, so they were deported and disappeared from history. The southern kingdom also corrupted God's teachings, and were subsequently also deported from their country, to be settled in what is now southern Iraq. Thus, the modern nation of Israel today is made up of descendants of only the few of the ancient Jews who returned after the Babylonian captivity. Herod tried to set himself up as the Messiah, and failed miserably, leading to the later final destruction of his temple and Jerusalem by the Romans (more on this in the description of the New Testament).

A seventh theme was that when even men of faith became powerful and successful in their own eyes, they often forgot how they got there and became corrupted by their own pride and indulgences. A couple of examples of individuals this happened to were Samson and Gideon in the book of Judges. Other examples were several of the kings of both Israel and Judah. The Old Testament also repeatedly demonstrates that not just kings but also how whole Biblical societies lost their way by either turning to other so-called gods or forgetting God altogether, and suffered severe consequences, mass murder, rape, pillaging, deportation, and the escape of only a remnant the people with only the clothes on their backs. Unfortunately, this appears to be happening today in parts of the Middle East just as depicted in the Old Testament. Our society today is noticeably turning to science, making gods of human intellect, and calling itself pluralistic, naming multiple gods and thinking of them as equal to the one God. We should all be taking note of what happened the Hebrews, recognize what is happening now in the Middle East and Africa, and realize it could happen here, too. The lesson in these examples is that people, no matter how successful, must always remain humble to recognize the God of the Old Testament as the one and only God, and thankful Him in all matters of life.

An eighth theme was that the pre-Christian people of the Bible were intelligent and literate, but basically savages by today's Christian standards. A requirement to prove a man was a member of the faithful was the surgical removal of part of his penis (circumcision). Abraham offered to kill his own son as a blood sacrifice. Jacob, Abraham's grandson, stole his twin brother's birthright, tricked his father into giving him the blessing that belonged to his brother, and stole livestock from his future father-in-law. Moses, the father of the Hebrew nation, killed an Egyptian man in cold blood. Joshua ordered the wipeout of whole towns and cities; men, women and children. King David, the most revered Old testament King, willfully killed and committed adultery on several occasions and got away with it, as did several of his subordinates, even though Hebrew law dictated the summary execution of anyone caught in murder or adultery. There were a significant number of people who (as a corruption of Hebrew law) practiced, as a form of worship, the sealing up their own children in clay jars and roasting them alive. The rule of society was vendetta, "an eye for an eye". And whole pre-Christian world was like this. While not in the Bible, in Greece, the most civilized of those pre-Christian societies, Socrates was forced to commit suicide simply because the rulers didn't like it that he told the truth. **This is one of the reasons that the teachings of Jesus in the New Testament were so unique, remarkable, and revolutionary. We now take for granted today many things that were totally foreign to even so-called civilized people in Old Testament times, primarily because of Christ's teachings.**

A ninth, and most important, theme was that there were consistent premonitions and then clear prophesies throughout the Old Testament that a new leader would emerge from the descendants of Abraham who would rule all the people of the earth. This ruler would variously be called the Messiah, Emanuel, or the Christ. And that his kingdom would not be geographic territory or an earthly throne, but would be in the hearts of men. The most familiar of these are the prophesies in the Book of Isaiah, but there are numerous intimations of this idea and concept from Genesis all the way through Malachi (the first and last books of the Old Testament).

A SYNOPSIS OF THE
NEW TESTAMENT

To fully comprehend the New Testament it must be understood that it whole theme is about one man, Jesus of Nazareth, his life, his teachings, his inheritance as the only real Son of the God of the Old Testament, his sacrifice as the "Passover Lamb" for the salvation of all who would believe in him, and the dramatic influence he had on his followers.

The Setting

In order to put the New Testament into proper perspective, it is important to understand the geophysical and cultural situation of the part of the world into which its main character, Jesus, was born and lived.

About 300 years of turmoil had passed for the Jewish people, by then called the nation of Judea, since Nehemiah had overseen the rebuilding of the city walls of Jerusalem. The Persian Empire had been defeated by the Greeks under Alexander the Great. Alexander had died and his kingdom had been split up and turned over to four of his minions, who each ruled his portion by force and intimidation. Descendants of the ruler that inherited the part of the Middle East that contained Judea were called the Seleucids, who were enemies of the Judean people and their religion.

About 100 years before Jesus was born, Judas Maccabeus led a successful revolt, which restored Judea as a separate kingdom. But in 63 BC, Pompey the Great sacked Jerusalem and made Judea part of the Roman Empire. The Romans then set up Judea as a Roman province, and placed it under the control of a puppet king, "Herod the Great". Herod decided that he was the promised "Messiah", the Christ prophesied in the Old Testament. He built several palaces and fortresses, and tore down and rebuilt the Temple on Mount Zion, bigger and better than the one built by Ezra and Nehemiah, and even the one originally built there by King Solomon. The ritual days of celebration, feasting, and sacrifices were reinstituted. In 49 BC Julius Caesar became Emperor and left Herod the Great in charge of Judea itself. The Jews, however, did not fully trust Herod because he was part Edomite, and thus not of true Jewish blood. Some of the more devout Jews withdrew to monasteries and set about to purify their worship and preserve the ancient Biblical writings. One of these groups was called the Essenes. One of the legacies of the Essenes was to preserve books of the Old Testament, among them the book of Isaiah. They were preserved on animal skins and hidden in caves in cliffs in a more desolate part of the Jordan valley overlooking the Dead Sea and only recently discovered. Another group, called the Zealots, were determined to throw off Roman rule and to restore Judea as a separate independent earthly nation.

Rome's approach to governing a province was strong but somewhat benign. Rome assigned a Roman governor to each province who only intervened on major issues, but who collected taxes for Rome, and stationed Roman soldiers in key locations around each province to keep order, and who's permission was necessary to administer the death penalty. The tax collection was contracted out to local citizens who had a fair amount of freedom on how they went about collecting those taxes. Some of them were unscrupulous, lining their own pockets and gaining a bad reputation for all such people. Also, the people from whom taxes were collected were without representation in the Roman government, which upset many people in Judea. Thus, the tax collectors were automatically considered sinners and breakers of the laws of Moses.

The day-to-day administering of the province was left to the local people. The province of Judea was governed by King Herod, but the city of Jerusalem was locally ruled by a religion-based organization called the Sanhedrin, made of two parties. Members of the more conservative party were called the Pharisees, who were in the majority at the time of Jesus' life. Members of the minority party were called the Sadducees. Since Judea was ruled as a theocracy, the main difference between the beliefs and policies of the two parties was that the Pharisees believed in life after death and the Sadducees didn't. However, both parties believed in strict adherence to the Old Testament laws and rituals, and considered anything else illegal and worthy of severe punishment, including death by stoning or torture. Jerusalem was the center of the Jewish faith, just like Mecca is today for the Muslims. Believers from all over the Roman Empire and beyond came there to worship on the numerous religious holidays. Many of these pilgrims spoke different languages; Latin, Greek, Persian, Aramaic, Hebrew, Gaelic, and a lot of other local dialects (this fact will become significant point in the book of Acts, described below).

When Julius Caesar had been assassinated in 44 BC, the Roman Empire passed to his nephew, Augustus Caesar. Augustus put down a major revolt led by Mark Anthony, and instituted a time of peace throughout the area, called the "Pax Romana", when people could safely travel, migrate, and trade throughout the empire. During this period, Herod's new temple had become the center of Jewish religious ritual, which included devout people coming from all over the known world to worship and offer sacrifices. The temple courtyard would have been a place of wholesale animal slaughter and burning of hundreds or even thousands of animals each day. It was probably a pretty bloody and smoky scene.

A few years into his rule, Augustus Caesar felt he needed to know the nature of the people he now ruled. So he decreed that a census be taken. One of the stipulations of the census was that the people must return to their ancestral homes to be counted. Thus, a young pregnant girl named Mary and the man she was engaged to, Joseph, traveled from Nazareth, their home town, near the Sea of Galilee in northern Judea, to Bethlehem, where Joseph's family came from. This is where the New Testament starts, with Jesus being born to Mary shortly after they arrived there. The Bible intimates that Jesus' family did not return to Nazareth after the census, but remained in Bethlehem. Note that Herod the Great died just a couple of years after Jesus was born, but not before he tried to have the baby Jesus killed by ordering the execution of all male children under 2 years old who lived in or around the town of Bethlehem. Joseph and Mary were divinely warned in advance of this slaughter and escaped temporarily to Egypt before the killings took place, and then later returned to Nazareth.

Also, the Jewish leaders had, about this time, created a supplement to the Torah, called the Talmud, providing much more detail about the practices of Jewish worship and sacrifice. It specifically defined how to practice the Sabbath, to dress, to eat, to bathe, to live, to travel, etc. It specified, among other things, just how far one could travel on the Sabbath Day and what constituted harvesting of food grains, making it a sin to break these rules on the Sabbath Day. And it made any breaking in these rules punishable as a major crime. This led to the beginnings of a movement that supported strict adherence to the Talmud rules and subequently would foment a hatred towards the followers of Jesus because he and his followers were accused of breaking some of these rules.

The institution of the Synagogue had been set up by then to provide a local building in each town and city where people could regularly go and worship each Sabbath, just like local churches today.

Now we begin the story of Jesus (as we deal with the 4 "gospels" as a group)

The first four books of the New Testament, **MATTHEW, MARK, LUKE, and JOHN**, are called the gospels. Each was written by a follower (disciple) of Jesus about the life of Jesus. They tell of his earthly life and ministry, including his teachings and the selection of a special group of twelve to assist him. Each of the authors had his own experiences and viewpoint and brought these into his document, sometimes with different emphasis on parts Jesus life and what he said and did. Some of the life events described in these books overlapped and some provided different slants on those events. Also, there were some items that were unique to a particular gospel. **Matthew** (sometimes called Levi) and **John** were two of the twelve men that accompanied and were taught directly by Jesus during his entire ministry. **Mark** was a Jewish convert to the "Way" (belief in the teachings and divinity of Jesus) but was not of the inner circle. However, he was friends with the twelve as well as Paul, and directly heard the stories about Jesus from them. Tradition says that he leaned most heavily on Peter's recollections in compiling his gospel. Peter was one of the twelve original disciples and had an action oriented personality. Thus, the gospel of Mark is more action oriented than the other gospels. **Luke** was not a Jew and was apparently not even present in Judea at the time of Jesus' ministry, but was rather an after-the-fact Greek convert to the "Way" under the tutelage and inspiration of Paul. (More about Paul later.)

Matthew (Levi), the person, was an accountant by training and had, before becoming a disciple, contracted out to the Roman Empire to collect taxes. He had an ordered, accounting mentality. Thus his gospel is generally grouped in sections by subject; (1) Jesus lineage and birth, early years, and preparation for his ministry, (2) his sermons and messages, (3) his miracles, (4) his parables (teaching allegories), (5) the healing miracles he performed, and (6) his execution and reappearance to the disciples. **Mark,** the person, was probably a young teenager during Jesus ministry. He apparently lived in Jerusalem when Peter was leading the church there, but had moved to Antioch, now in northern Lebanon, when he began writing his gospel, setting down the words of the apostles. The book of Mark starts off with the beginnings of Jesus' adult ministry and emphasizes Jesus' actions and activities, basically in the order they occurred, just as Peter, a man of action, would have done. **Luke** was a medical doctor, scientist, and a traveling companion of **Paul** during much of Paul's ministry. His approach was that of a researcher, who studied the precepts of the Jewish faith and probably most clinically and precisely depicted the origins and ideals of the "Way", and the life, ministry, execution, and resurrection [return to life] of Jesus, from the aspect of the Jewish traditions and prophesies. His account of Jesus birth in Luke chapter 2 is the most recognized by most people. **John** was one of the most inner circle of Jesus disciples. His depiction of Jesus is on a most personal and detailed basis. He considered himself Jesus closest human friend and often refers to himself as the "beloved disciple". He is specially detailed in the accounts of Jesus trial, execution and resurrection.

All four gospels document the Lord's Supper, the last meal before Jesus was crucified, and clearly identifies it as the "final Passover" and proposes that the body and blood of Christ is the ultimate replacement for the Jewish animal and blood sacrifices. And all of the four gospels irrevocably declare that Jesus is the Son of God, the Christ and Messiah promised in the Old Testament and the redeemer of mankind, and the only way to eternal life. Two of the gospels document the prayer called the Lord's Prayer, (Matthew and Luke) that Jesus taught as a model and example of how believers should pray.

Also, all four of these books contain so much valuable information about Jesus life, the miracles the Christ performed, rules for living and for worship, and promises of grace through Christ, that this synopsis cannot even begin to scratch the surface. One needs to read them all **in detail** to see proof of both Jesus Christ's humanity and divinity, and to understand the real meaning of Christ-like living and the promise of eternal life.

Additional gospel detail (as we deal with the 4 gospels individually)

The gospel of **Matthew** begins by introducing us to Jesus' earthly lineage, tracing his ancestry from Abraham though King David and onward, to prove he was a pure Jew on his mother's side. He explains Jesus' virgin birth and the visit of the Three Wise Men who were familiar with the Old Testament prophesies and who came from the "east", probably from the area that is now southern Iraq (who just might have been descendants of the Jewish people who had been deported by Nebuchadnezzar but who had not returned to rebuild Jerusalem with Ezra or Nehemiah). Matthew then documents the advent of John the Baptist as the person who first baptized Jesus and introduced him to the world. Next, he documents the collection of Jesus teachings including one section called the Beatitudes, a series of what today sounds like benign, loving statements. But to the world of Jesus day, were a radical departure from its semi-savage concepts of existence, leadership, eye-for-an-eye interpersonal relationships, and worship practices. Instead of sounding caring and loving to the Jewish leadership, it most likely angered many, especially the traditionalists who didn't want to change their thinking. He also said that every detail of the Old Testament law was still in effect and people were still condemned for even thoughts of evil and not just acts. And in Matthew, Jesus summarized the Ten Commandments into two statements as follows: **"You shall love the Lord your God with all your heart and with all your soul and with all your mind. This is the first and great commandment** (a condensation of the first 4). **And the second is like it: You shall love your neighbor as yourself** (a condensation of the last 6)." With this statement Jesus turned the Ten Commandments from simply a set of laws to be followed in ones actions, into a full internal commitment of one's heart and soul and mind to them as part of one's whole being. The style of this gospel is a thorough, detailed document, and thus should appeal best to the accountant or business person.

As said earlier, **Mark** basically describes the actions and activities of Jesus, from the start of his ministry until his death on the cross. It begins with his ministry in Nazareth, his home town in northern Judea, where his family must have returned after escaping the slaughter of children in Bethlehem. It then tells of his travels around the country of Judea, preaching, teaching and performing remarkable miracles. In addition to Jesus actions, it also includes additional clarifications of the teachings of Jesus. It records that Jesus selected twelve men from among his followers to become his students. Interestingly, two of those he selected were apparently of the party of the "Zealots", including Judas Iscariot, who betrayed him to the Jewish leaders. It also particularly details the impetuous nature of Peter as a disciple. It is well worth reading in full to get an idea of what kind of man Jesus was; self assured, strong, wise, charismatic, and at the same time humble. And it states strongly the Jesus had the power to miraculously heal people of all sorts of physical and mental maladies. This gospel most likely speaks best to the action oriented person who wants to know and understand what happened during Jesus' life and ministry.

Luke is a chronological history of the birth, life, death, and resurrection of Jesus. It is precise in its descriptions, and is best know for the depiction of Jesus' birth in a livestock barn in Bethlehem. It is the source of the well known story about the angels appearing to the shepherds on the night of his birth, and those shepherds' visit to Jesus, who had been placed in a livestock feeding trough (manger) by Mary his mother. It documents both his teachings and his miracles, repeating many of the same teaching, miracles and events described in Matthew. Luke repeats the Lord's Prayer also found in Matthew. He also documents Jesus' prediction that the nation of Judea and the Temple built by King Herod would be totally destroyed. (This happened about 50 years after Christ was killed. And the temple, the center of Jewish worship, was never rebuilt.) Luke ends with Jesus' words of encouragement to his disciples after his resurrection from the dead, and his ascension into heaven. This gospel should appeal best to the professional, the engineer, and the scientist.

The Gospel of **John** begins with a statement that says "In the beginning was Word, and the Word was with God, and the Word was God", **irrevocably stating that Jesus, the redeemer, and God, the creator, are one.** It seems to be the most personal depiction of Jesus' calling to the original twelve disciples to follow him. One of the most famous passages in the Bible is John 3:1-21, which in some ways condenses much of the message of Jesus into a few short paragraphs. The book continues to explain the divinity of Jesus and his gift of eternal life to all who believe in him. Jesus is displayed as both strong and assured, declaring "I have come into the world as light, so that whoever believes in me may not remain in darkness". And then, only a few verses later he does something very humble. He washes the feet of his disciples. This book has the most details of the trials of Jesus just before he was crucified. **Something that all the gospels document, but especially John, was the declaration by Jesus that his kingdom was not of this world but in heaven and in the hearts of men (contrary to the concept of many Jews of that time that he would set up an earthly kingdom).** This gospel probably best speaks to those who want to get acquainted with Jesus as a real person and a man of God.

> **The rest of the New Testament is a record of the events and teachings of the followers of Jesus after his death and resurrection**

<u>ACTS</u> is the next book immediately following the gospels, and holds a unique place in the New Testament. It is the book of the history of the next forty years of the establishment and spread of Christianity throughout the Roman Empire. It was written by Luke, the same author who wrote the gospel of **Luke**. It starts with some of the disciples still believing that Jesus would immediately return, set up an earthly kingdom and get rid of Roman rule. However, Jesus had clearly said that instead, the disciples would "receive power" to be "witnesses" (not warriors) to carry his message to the world. Next the disciples picked a replacement for Judas (one of the twelve disciples who had betrayed Jesus). But just as the people in the Old Testament picked Saul to be their king instead of letting God do it, the individual the remaining disciples picked was not the right one. That person made no further mark on history. Then suddenly about 40 days after Jesus' death, on the day of "Pentecost", the "Holy Spirit" came over the group of disciples in Jerusalem. They quit being students (disciples) and became teachers (apostles). Peter suddenly became a great orator and expounder of the "Way" to the Jerusalem Jews, winning over thousands people, 3000 at one time, to be believers in Jesus. The other disciples, just as suddenly, were able to speak languages that were not their own but were the languages of visitors to Jerusalem from other countries, so they could tell of Jesus to them as well, in their own languages and dialects. Peter and other apostles were arrested for speaking out about Jesus and for proclaiming him as the promised Messiah. They were grilled by the Sanhedrin, but were let go. All the new believers sold all their possessions and put the money in a common pool. And they spent their whole time living communally, eating and worshiping. They seemed to still be expecting Jesus to come back right away to set up an "earthly" kingdom. Seven men were selected to bring order and serve

the converts while the apostles were spreading the word. These were the first deacons. One of these was Steven, who was arrested, convicted of religious treason and was stoned to death, becoming the first martyr. One of the supporters of the stoning was a man named Saul. He was a young, highly educated Pharisee was a strong proponent of the Jewish law, and who was intelligent, well educated in all aspects of the Jewish faith and traditions, and proficient in several of the languages of the day. To add to his resume, he had been awarded Roman Citizenship, a significant honor that would protect him and his later ministry as a Christian. However, before he became a Christian he decided to become dedicated to the eradication of the new "Way" because it, in his mind, conflicted with Jewish faith and tradition.

Saul went about systematically arresting the local Jews and throwing them in prison. Then he heard that there was a strong group of believers in the city Damascus, a city about a hundred miles north of Jerusalem. So he obtained letters of introduction to the city authorities and went there to bring the believers back in chains to be prosecuted in Jerusalem. But on the way there, he had a dramatic, life changing experience. He was blinded by a powerful light and knocked to the ground, and Jesus himself spoke to him. Jesus asked him why he was being persecuted, and directed Saul follow him instead of persecuting his followers. Saul remained blind for several days, and his sight was restored by a believer who was told by Jesus to help Saul, even though he had a reputation for arresting believers.

Saul then went off by himself to figure out what to do. His name was changed to Paul, and after that he went into exile in Tarsus in what is now southern Turkey. About this time, a group of strong believers in the city of Antioch in what is now northern Lebanon, organized themselves into the first Christian "church", and there for the first time were called "Christians". Some of the church leaders had heard about Paul's conversion and went to Tarsus to invite Paul to move to Antioch and join them. He did, and started effectively preaching for the very cause to which he had once been so ardently opposed. Because of his extensive training in Jewish history, tradition and prophecies, he was very effective in explaining that Jesus was the Christ who had come just as the Old

Testament predicted. (**Thus, it appears that Paul became <u>God's</u> choice as the twelfth apostle.**)

In Antioch he teamed up with others from that church and went from town to town throughout what is now southern and central Turkey and also into Greece, leading many, both Jew and non-Jew (Gentile) to become believers, and organized local churches wherever he went. He started most visits by going to the Jewish synagogues to teach. But for the most part, he was far more successful with Gentiles than with Jews, because the Jews were so tied into their traditions and rituals they couldn't accept that Jesus was the Messiah, even though Paul was able to prove it by quoting the Old Testament prophecies. He also preached in Athens, the center of Greek learning. But unfortunately, there his message was just treated as another of many philosophies. He was unable there to get his message over that Jesus was the one and only way to God and salvation, something he would mention in his later letters. In some places he even innocently caused riots because of his teachings. He was thrown into jail several times but was always released, in some cases miraculously, and he was stoned and left for dead at least once, but survived. He never gave up, and left a legacy of numerous local churches throughout the areas that are now Turkey and Greece, which became the core of the worldwide expansion of Christianity.

The last part of **Acts**, tells about Paul's return to Jerusalem and his acceptance by Peter and other apostles there. But it also tells of plots by the Zealots to kill him. They caused a riot, and Paul had to be taken into custody by Roman soldiers to protect him. Because Paul was a Roman citizen, he was able to preach to both Herod Antipas, who was by this time the successor to Herod the Great and king of Judea, and also to two successive Roman governors of Judea. Then he was taken to Rome, where he appears to have led many more conversions, wrote several of the letters that appear in the New Testament, and, according to tradition, lived several more years, sometimes under arrest and other times free to travel. But also according to tradition, he was eventually executed by the Roman Emperor.

Paul was undoubtedly the most influential of all the apostles in changing belief in Jesus from being just a Jewish sect into the most widespread religion in the world.

While on Paul's travels, he wrote a number of letters to the churches where he had previously preached or planned to visit. He also wrote three letters of advice to two younger preachers (1st Timothy, 2nd Timothy and Titus), one to a slave owner (Philemon), and one to the Jews in Jerusalem (Hebrews). There may have been other letters by Paul. However, the ones in the Bible are those that the early churches considered important enough that they were preserved for 300 years, and included in the Bible. These letters of Paul make up much of the rest of New Testament, as follows:

The book of **ROMANS** is the first of Paul's several letters to appear in the Bible, but not the first one he wrote. Rome was the capital of the Roman Empire, most powerful empire in the world at the time. The book was written to the believers in Rome, apparently because Paul planned to visit there. Its style is interesting in that it seems to follow inductive logic patterns established by the Greek philosophers. I suspect that he used this method to particularly reach the people of Rome who were normally well educated and versed in Greek culture and history. Unlike other letters, it was written to the Christians in Rome before Paul actually went there. He starts off by complimenting the Roman believers, and reaffirming his own beliefs in the resurrected Christ and his promise of eternal life. He then condemns all kinds of sins including so-called intellectuals who egotistically trust their own logic rather than the Biblical truths, those who worship the creations rather than the creator, unbridled sexual practices (and particularly homosexuality), as well as a whole other list of ungodly thoughts and actions. He lets all know that everyone can't help doing wrong and must have Christ in their hearts as atonement for those wrongs and as a sacrifice for their sins. Two passages in **Romans** that I particularly like are "And we know that for those who love God, all things work together for good....". And also, "...neither death, nor life, nor angels, nor rulers, nor things present, nor things to come, nor powers, nor height, nor depth, nor anything else in all creation, will be able to separate us from the love of God in Christ Jesus our lord." He also makes it appear quite simple for people to become believers and to be loved by God when he says **"...if you confess with your mouth that Jesus is Lord and believe in your heart that God raised him from the dead, you will be saved."** Of course the easy part is confessing with one's mouth. The hard part is really believing in one's heart.

Paul's second letter in the Bible is **1ˢᵗ CORINTHIANS.** Corinth was a wealthy trade city in Greece with lots of illegal activities and morality problems. Paul spent some time there preaching and teaching. But other preachers had been there as well. In this letter he shows particular concern that the Christians there would start to worship one preacher or another instead of Jesus Christ, and would create divisions in the church. He also expresses concern that people would wrongly think they are too smart to believe in Christ. He tells church members to avoid sexual immorality and that a marriage should be between one man and one woman. He explains that church members should not drag each other into court but settle their disputes as loving Christians. He also says that preachers can be married, and also to get paid by the church. He says divorce and remarriage are not good ideas except in very unusual circumstances, and offers guides as to the roles of husbands and wives in a marriage. And he admonishes everyone to do their best, even if they can't be perfect or win a race. He states that the Lord's Supper (Communion) is a serious business and should be done reverently. And he explains that different people in the church have different abilities and talents, and no one should be looked down on because he is different. The thirteenth chapter of **1ˢᵗ Corinthians** is a very moving and beautiful ode to love and understanding, that all should read over and over again. Paul warns against speaking in tongues unless there is someone present who can understand and interpret what is being said. **He states also that if we believe in Jesus Christ and that he was raised from the dead, we will be raised from the dead also.**

2ⁿᵈ CORINTHIANS is a follow-on letter, where Paul says, among other things, that it is more important to praise and thank God than to condemn others. He says to not boast or brag about yourself but let God commend you. But he also states that believers can be bold in the preaching of the gospel and must be persistent in it, even if they suffer persecution as a result. He also warns against false teachers who can corrupt the faith. In both letters to the Corinthians, Paul asks for donations for the believers in Jerusalem, who by this time had become poor and were by this time under all sorts of persecution.

GALATIANS is a letter written to the believers in what is now southern and central Turkey. It was one of the first areas visited by Paul when he decided to go out from Antioch to make converts in other towns, and was probably one of the first letters he wrote. He wrote it mostly to Jewish converts. He says in this letter that the Law (based on the Ten Commandments) is our "guardian" to shape our conscience and guide for us, to determine what is right and wrong, and to let us know that no one can be fully good. But then Jesus Christ came to be our blood sacrifice (Passover lamb), **so that we could be justified (made sinless) by our faith in him**, not by strict obedience to the Old Testament law and not even by good works. And he states that in that faith, all believers are equal, no distinction between Jew and Greek, master and slave, male and female. And also that the former Jewish laws are still vital as moral and ethical guides, but that the Jewish rituals and symbolism (including circumcision) are no longer of any special value. He also states in this letter the ways in which a Christian, if truly a Christian, would naturally think and act. They are called "the fruits of the spirit", as follows: "**... love, joy, peace, patience, kindness, goodness, faithfulness, gentleness, and self-control**". These are the important traits that identify those who are true believers. He also says that if anyone is having a moral or ethical problem, fellow believers should try to help that individual and not just ignore or condemn.

The next of Paul's letters is **EPHESIANS**. Ephesus was a large and rich, basically Greek port city on the west end of modern day Turkey. It had a well designed sanitary sewer system and a great library containing writings from all over the known world. But its greatest claim to fame was that it was the center of worship of the Greek goddess Artemis. There was a huge temple for Artemis there that looked very much like the Parthenon in Athens. Artemis was a goddess of female sex and power. There was a guild of artisans in Ephesus who had become rich by making silver images of Artemis and selling them to the pilgrims who visited the temple. Then Paul showed up offering a new religion where there were no images to be made, only belief in a crucified and risen Christ, who offered eternal life. And all this new religion took was not sacrifices or sacraments or good works, but only trust and faith. He said that one is **"...saved by faith, and not of works, lest any man should boast"**. And again as before, he says that all people are equal in Christ. In this letter he also gives instructions as to the roles of husbands, wives and, this time, children, in a marriage. And he says that one should wear his faith like armor to protect against the forces of evil. His teaching caused a riot in the city, fomented primarily by the silversmiths who were afraid that people would turn away from Artemis and no longer buy their statues. Paul was arrested and thrown in prison but soon released. So, he was able to stay in Ephesus for a while longer, teaching and preaching. Paul made several references to himself being in chains when he wrote this letter, so it is assumed he was in prison in Rome when he wrote it.

A hundred or so years after Paul left Ephesus, the commercial harbor there silted up, moving the seacoast five miles away from the city. Also, an earthquake destroyed the temple of Artemis which was never rebuilt, and Ephesus became a ghost town.

The next of Paul's letters is **PHILLIPPIANS**. Philippi was a city in northern Greece named after Phillip of Macedon, father of Alexander the Great. Passages in the book of Acts provide several interesting happenings on Paul's visit to Philippi. Philippi apparently didn't have synagogue, so Paul went to a nearby stream to teach where women went out to wash their clothes. He immediately made a convert of one of leading ladies of the city. But Paul later lead to Christ a slave girl who was a mystic, and she lost her powers when converted. She had been making money for her owners, so they brought false charges against Paul and had him arrested. But while he was in jail he converted the jailer and his whole family to belief in Christ.

The letter to the Philippians was written later when Paul was in a prison in Rome to encourage the Philippians in their faith. The book of Philippians is full of beautiful and insightful statements by Paul. Some are as follows: His personal confession **"for me to live is Christ and to die is gain"**, his admonition to converts, you must **"work out your own salvation with fear and trembling, for it is God who works in you..."**, and closes with the admonition **"...whatever is true, whatever is honorable, whatever is just, whatever is pure, whatever is lovely, whatever is commendable, if there is any excellence, if there is anything worthy of praise, think on these things"**.

After the book of Philippians in the Bible is Paul's letter to Colossi. This was a city in what is now central Turkey. Paul wrote the letter to the **COLOSSIANS**, primarily to strengthen them against the Judaizers who insisted that new Christians follow Jewish rituals such as circumcision. He also warned them to be weary of philosophers who wanted people to question everything and commit to nothing, and also those who said that you could sin all you felt like and still be saved (thus making the Ten Commandments and Jesus' moral teachings of no value). He tells the Colossians to put away what is earthly in them **"...sexual immorality, impurity, evil desire, envy, and worship of wealth and position"** and to adopt **"...compassionate hearts, kindness, humility, meekness, and patience..."**. He again tells husbands to love their wives, that wives should submit to their husbands, and that fathers should encourage their children to do well. He also tells those who are in slavery that they should do well in whatever their situation, because they are working for God and not their masters. And masters must treat their slaves justly and as equal human beings, because they have the same master in heaven.

Thessalonica was a city in northern Greece. Paul wrote two letters, **1st and 2nd THESSALONIANS** to the church there. These were most likely two of the earliest letters he wrote. The first one praised the Christians of Thessalonica for their continued faith in God and the Christian message. He tells them not to be concerned about believers who have already died because they will be raised from the dead just as was Jesus Christ. He also admonishes them to have respect for the people who help out in the church, and to hold fast to the good and abstain from every form of evil. In his second letter he warns against anyone who believes he is above the law and acts as if he is a God. And Paul asks that believers hold onto their faith, even in the face of adversity. In both letters Paul lets believers know that, for certainty, Christ will return, but that believers are not to sit around and wait, but to stay busy with both doing good and with their normal activities and professions. Paul used himself as an example in that while in Thessalonica he worked as a tent maker to pay his own way.

Paul wrote two letters to Timothy a young convert and a protégé of Paul. These letters provide instructions on how to be a good preacher and church leader. At the time of the writing of **1ˢᵗ TIMOTHY**, Timothy was the pastor of the church at Ephesus. Paul told him that the law is good in that it identifies the difference between right and wrong. He said to avoid people in the church who would cause dissention and question the teachings of Christ. He emphasized the need for prayer without anger or quarreling, even prayer for kings and people in high places. He instructed Timothy on how to pick church leaders and deacons, and that men (with one wife) should be selected for those positions. He said not to discriminate between people because of their age but have respect for all, and be an example in love and moral living for all. And that the people of the church should make sure that if someone in the church was suspected of wrongdoing, that the evidence should be fully analyzed to insure it is true before bringing a charge. He also told Timothy to not be swayed by those who would question or distort the teachings of Christ, but stick to the truth that Jesus was the promised Christ, and that through his crucifixion, all people who believe in him would be saved and have eternal life.

In **2ⁿᵈ TIMOTHY** Paul wrote to Timothy from prison in Rome. He told Timothy not to be ashamed of Paul's imprisonment. He also said to be a good soldier for God, and told him that all information in the Bible **"...is good for teaching, for reproof and correction, and for training in righteousness"**. He also warned Timothy that **"...the time is coming when people will not listen to sound teaching, but instead listen to**

teachers that suit their own passions, and wander off into myths", (sounds like what is happening today).

<u>TITUS</u> was another of Paul's apprentices. He had been sent by Paul to teach and lead believers in Crete. (Crete is a large island in the Mediterranean south of Greece where the Minoan civilization once existed. However, that culture had decayed and the people had lost their way.) In the book of **Titus**, Paul warned him that the Cretans were now lazy and good for very little, but that if Titus sticks to the message of **"Christ and Him Crucified"** he will be successful. Like in his letters to Timothy, he instructed Titus in how to pick good church leaders and what their qualifications should be. He also reminded Titus to show integrity, dignity, and sound speech so that opponents couldn't hold him up to ridicule. He also reminded Titus that all believers should be above reproach, even slaves to their masters. Also, he told Titus to remind his people to be submissive and obedient to rulers and authorities and to speak evil of no-one (hard to do).

<u>PHILEMON</u> was to a rich person and a slave owner. He was also a convert to Christianity. One of his slaves, Onesimus, had run away and gone to Rome. Paul met him there and won him also over to Christ. Paul wrote a letter to **Philemon** telling him of the conversion of Onesimus and his willingness to go back to Philemon and become his slave again. Paul, in this letter, also told Philemon to take Onesimus back without punishment and also to receive him as a brother in Christ just as he would receive Paul. This is a good lesson today for CEOs and managers of companies and corporations to treat their employees fairly, and respectfully.

The last letter by Paul in the Bible is **<u>HEBREWS</u>.** Some scholars don't believe Paul wrote it, because differences in style. But it must be remembered that Paul was a Jew and Pharisee, as well as a very educated man. He was writing here to his own people, who are also well educated in Jewish history, laws, rituals, prophesies, and tradition. In **Hebrews**, Paul appealed to their knowledge by quoting prophesies from the Old Testament which predicted the coming of Christ, and that the Christ was to be not an earthly king, but rather a ruler of our hearts and a provider of salvation and eternal life (something the Zealots didn't want to hear).

The Jews highly honored and respected Moses as the founder of their nation and their culture. But Paul said that Jesus was not just a founder of a nation but was higher than Moses in that he was a high priest of the order of Melchisedek. Melchisedek was the priest to Abraham, Moses ancestor (a fact known to educated Jews), and about whom there is a mystery of both his beginning and end. He said that the contract between Jesus (the Christ) and all humanity is also higher than the agreement that Moses had from God in creating the Hebrew nation (something that the Jewish leaders also did not want to hear). He pointed out that the extensive sacrifices that were required of the Jewish people are no longer necessary, as the blood of Christ is the be all and end all of such sacrifices. But what is instead required is true commitment in heart and mind to belief in Jesus Christ, his teachings and the sacrifice of his own life. He warned the followers of Jesus not to be weary of their calling but to stay on course even in the face of ridicule and punishment.

The next letter was not written by Paul. Instead its author was **JAMES**, the younger half brother of Jesus. (There was a James who was one of the original 12 disciples, but he was apparently one of the early martyrs, arrested by Zealots or other Jewish leaders, or even maybe by Paul himself before his conversion.) James, though not one of the twelve Apostles, had become a leader in the Jerusalem church. In his letter, he wrote mainly to Jewish converts in Jerusalem and other areas, to tell them that belief in and worship of Christ is not enough (and basically dead) if it does not lead to good works. He reminded followers that Christ taught <u>two</u> basic commandments. One was to love God with all your heart, soul, and mind. But the other, just as important, was to love your neighbor just as you love yourself. He said that righteousness is not complete without both. He also said that one should not try to be wise without belief, but believe first and one will become wise. In addition he said not to favor one person over another but to treat all as equals. He also said to control one's tongue, because what you say can be very hurtful to others. In addition he said to not be concerned about tomorrow but to take one day at a time and be happy in it, and to hang in there even if things go bad.

Peter, one of the chosen twelve disciples, wrote the next two letters that are preserved in the New Testament. 1ˢᵗ **PETER** opens with one of the great statements of the Bible, **"Blessed be the God and Father of our Lord Jesus Christ! According to his great mercy, that he has caused us to be born again to a living hope through the resurrection of Jesus Christ from the dead, to an inheritance that in imperishable, undefiled, and unfading, kept in heaven for you...(the believers)"**. He said that Christ is a living stone, and the corner stone of the new order, but also a stumbling stone to those who refuse to believe. He said to put away all malice, deceit, hypocrisy, envy, and slander. He said to submit to earthly governments and leaders, even those we have concerns about. He reiterated Paul's admonitions to husbands and wives in their complimentary roles in a marriage, and that each should help and support the other in their beliefs. He said that each Christian has a responsibility to support other Christians in their sufferings and at the same time to be humble **"...under the mighty hand of God..."**. (One should read this book while visualizing Peter standing before a crowd speaking this letter as a sermon. It is a powerful message.)

2ⁿᵈ **PETER** opens with the statement that Peter sees himself as both **"...a servant and apostle of Jesus Christ..."**. He made sure the readers and hearers of this letter knew that he was an eye witness to Jesus and could speak with authority on Jesus' teachings and divinity. He said to watch out for false teachers who will call the divinity of Christ a myth and will cast doubt on Jesus' basic teachings. He said that the purveyors of these falsehoods will be condemned to hell. He also told believers to be confident that Jesus Christ will come again, and to be prepared without impurity and at peace with all. And in addition he said that the world would be destroyed by fire, but to those who are getting impatient, please recognize that to God "...one day is a thousand years and a thousand years is one day." In other words, he indicated that time as we count it does not have the same meaning to God. And that we must be patient. Peter also said that "The day of the Lord will come like a thief in the night..." So, it appears that Peter is saying that believers are only deluding themselves when they try to predict when it will happen. (Again, this book sounds like a sermon.) Both letters by Peter emphasize the power and majesty of God and his earthly presence, Jesus Christ.

John, also one of original twelve disciples, in addition to the gospel of John, wrote three of the letters that appear after Peter's letters as books in the New Testament. **1ˢᵗ JOHN** opens with a statement by John that he was speaking from first hand knowledge, because he was an eye witness to the advent of Jesus Christ. He said that there is no mystery in God, because he is "truth" and "light", and when we do not live our daily lives in this knowledge we are in darkness and there is no light in us. He also said that if we say we have no wrong in us we are **liars**. He told his readers that we need to recognize that we are sinners and to recognize and confess those sins to God. And if we confess those sins, believing in the saving grace of Jesus Christ, God will forgive them. He warned against "Antichrists", people who do not have the truth in them and who deny that Jesus is the Christ. He also stated firmly that "God is Love" and that Jesus Christ represents that love. John also assured believers that with their belief they are guaranteed eternal life.

2ⁿᵈ and 3ʳᵈ JOHN are letters written by the apostle John to individuals congratulating both on their belief and commitment. In each he reiterated that God is Love and warned the readers to watch out for deceivers who deny the bodily return of Christ in the last days. In **3ʳᵈ John** he specifically warned about one particular individual who "...likes to put himself first." And that this individual was trying to put some local believers out of the church because they welcomed and were friendly to other believers not part of the local congregation. It is a strong lesson opposing discrimination and bigotry especially within the church itself and between denominations.

The letter of **JUDE** is the next to the last book of the Bible. In it the author identified himself as the younger brother of James, probably the one who wrote the book of James. He specifically warned against people who have come into churches who "... are grumblers, malcontents, following their own sinful desires, and who are loud-mouthed boasters, showing favoritism to gain advantage." Then **Jude** told believers to "... build yourselves up in your faith and pray in the Holy Spirit, and keep yourselves in the love of God, waiting for the mercy of our lord Jesus Christ that leads to eternal life."

The last book of the Bible is **REVELATION**. It was written by John the apostle, who also wrote the **Gospel of John** and the letters; **1st, 2nd, and 3rd John**. By the time he wrote **Revelation** he was old, probably in his 90s, and a prisoner in a jail on the island of Patmos off the southwestern coast of Turkey. He called himself by then **"John the Elder"**, apparently indicating both his age and his leadership in the faith. It is a book of prophesy, helping believers to look into the future. It has a lot of symbolism that needs to be interpreted in the light of the rest of the Bible. Otherwise, significant misinterpretations can take place. For instance, many have used it to predict the precise date for the end of the world, something **Peter** specifically warned against.

The book starts with greeting to seven Christian churches that were in what is now modern Turkey. Some he praised, others he condemned and some he had both good and bad words for, and told them what they needed to do to straighten out. He then began a series of prophecies filled with symbolism. He described a visit to heaven and to the throne of God. He then explained that Jesus was the "Lamb of God", God's son but also the Passover sacrifice, and as such, worthy of great praise and honor. He then saw Jesus, the Lamb of God, open seven seals that predicted the events in the process of the end of the world. He described how the chosen people would be protected while all others would be subject to pain and death. He described a pregnant woman who could have been Mary, Jesus mother, or could have been the nation of Israel/Judah/Judea giving birth to Christianity. He described the devil, in several beastly forms, who would try to kill the woman and her son, and he warned of the severe consequences of devil worship. He variously described the culture of the non-believing world as "the great prostitute" and "Babylon". He also described how Christ would come again, this time on a white horse to judge the world, and that the devil would be defeated, and the condemned would be "thrown into the lake of fire". Then he ended the book by foretelling of a new and reborn heaven and earth, and that God and Christ would be physically present in it, and would be honored and worshiped by all people. The last sentence of the Bible says **"The grace of the Lord Jesus be with all, Amen."**

Themes of the New Testament.

The first and foremost theme was the proof and assurance that Jesus is the Christ, the Messiah promised and prophesied about in the Old Testament. This is testified over and over again by the quotes from Jesus' own testimony, the gospel writers, and by the people who were present during and immediately after his appearance on earth.

The second theme is that Jesus and God are one, not two separate entities, that Jesus is the "Voice" of God as well as an ultimate demonstration of his love for all people through his healing ministry, earthly suffering, and death on the cross. Thus, Christians believe in one God, not two or more as claimed by some current Jews and Muslims. Jesus himself said so, as well his followers. This is also consistent with the assertion that when Jesus was conceived, Mary, his earthly mother, was a virgin, and that his father was God the creator, as prophesied by Isaiah 700 years before Jesus was born.

The third theme was that Jesus brought a whole new and revolutionary way of believing and living, that was basically contrary to the accepted standards of the time. He first said that he did not come into the world to replace the "Law", and that all the crimes and sins condemned in the Old Testament were still crimes and sins, even if one doesn't do them but just <u>thinks</u> about doing them. Thus, no-one is sinless or pure, and is automatically condemned. But he also said that he came into world not to condemn the world, but that the world might be <u>saved</u> through him, and that in belief, one's sins are "washed white as snow". His approach was to not just follow the "don'ts" of the Ten Commandments, but to turn these "don'ts" into "dos". For example, he said that there were really only two commandments, "Love the Lord your God with all your heart, soul and mind, but also love your neighbor as yourself". He defined "neighbor" as anyone, especially those who showed or needed love and compassion, but also even non-believers and one's enemies. This meant that one should not discriminate or be bigoted. One should try to help others in the best ways possible. One should not just do what is asked but "if one is asked to carry a load a mile, go the second mile". Be honest, open and humble, but also be strong and prepared, and educated in the word and sure of one's faith; to protect ones-self and other believers from backsliding or corruption, and to make believers into effective witnesses.

The fourth theme was that Jesus died on a Roman cross but also came back to life on the third morning to prove that he had conquered death and could give eternal life to believers. Thus, Christians changed the celebration of the day of worship (the Sabbath) from the traditional seventh day of the week (Saturday) (a day of rest) to the first day of the week (Sunday), to celebrate the day of Jesus' return to life, and to recognize the beginning of God's new kingdom. Jesus himself had said the "The Sabbath was made for man and not man for the Sabbath."

The fifth theme was that Jesus said emphatically that he did not come to set up an earthly kingdom, but that his kingdom would be in the human heart, and that believers should go out as witnesses to his message (and not as conquerors).

The sixth theme was that Jesus said that an entity that would become part of the human heart and soul, who would follow him who would variously be called the Holy Ghost, the Holy Spirit, the Spirit of the Living God, who would live in peoples' hearts and would help people believe in Christ, to see the truth, to be enthusiastic about their faith, and to act as a right conscience. The presence of this new spirit was graphically demonstrated on the day of Pentecost, 40 days after Jesus died. This spirit seems apparent even in today's society represented by strong adherents to the faith even in this age of scientific reason that tries to explain everything by logic and experiment only, and to discount faith.

The seventh theme is that Christ would be followed by many others who would claim to be the Christ or the savior of the world, but that they would not be, and would be recognized for the crimes they would commit against others, for their attempts to distort the truth of the Bible and its teachings, or for what they would avoid doing in worshiping God or helping others. In other words there would be many little "anti-Christs". However, before the return of the true Christ, there would be a seemingly all powerful final anti-Christ that would be very popular among people but would turn out to be the devil himself.

The eighth theme is that even people who have a heart for helping others may be doing the right thing but for the wrong reasons, unless their reasons for doing right for others is based on their belief and worship of God. But also those who worship God but do not have a heart to help others are automatically not real believers in Christ and his teachings. There is a name given to these (Secular Humanists), who may receive the satisfaction of helping others, but who most likely will not teach the value in helping, nor would they not accrue to themselves the promise of eternal life

The ninth theme is that the New Testament recognized only two rituals and considered all others no longer valid (including circumcision). The first ritual was the Lord's Supper (that replaced the Old Testament Passover). Jesus specifically said "Do this in remembrance of me" in order to ritually demonstrate acceptance of Jesus blood and his body as the once-for-all sacrifice for sins. The second was baptism. While Jesus did not specifically say to do this, he set the example for it by being baptized by John the Baptist when he began his earthy ministry. Christ's followers seemed to consider it part of the process of becoming a Christian (see in Acts when the Apostle Phillip led the Ethiopian Eunuch to Christ). Some Christian denominations consider it only an outward symbol of the one's inward conversion and the start of a new life in Christ, as it is not mentioned as a requirement in Paul's letters. Others consider it essential to salvation. (This difference seems to come from the differing interpretation of the gospel of John chapter 3 verse 5 where Jesus refers to birth by "...water and the spirit". However, Jesus goes on to use the term "flesh" in a follow-on statement, indicating that he is referring to physical birth, not water baptism.) Also, some consider baptism should be done at birth (commonly called Christening). Others believe it should be done only after one confesses belief in Christ. But all assume it needs to be done as part of the process to identify that the new believer is entering the new Christian life and becoming a recognized part of the community of believers.

Some early Jewish converts to Christianity believed that all male converts should be circumcised. However, the apostle Paul denounced this, saying this was not necessary to becoming a Christian. New Testament writers did tell believers not to eat food that had been offered to idols, but this was to indicate to others that a Christian did not acknowledge those other gods, and early Christians were also told it was O.K. to not eat kosher. On at least one occasion, Jesus washed the feet of his disciples, but did not ask his disciples to do so, but only to be humble. Although the apostle Paul said that he thought it was probably better to be celibate, he did not tell Christians that they must be, and the apostle Peter, considered the first leader of the Christian faith, was married. One Christian sect today practices snake handling. However, there is nothing in the Bible that supports this as a ritual.

The tenth theme is that once a believer becomes a true believer, he is protected by God in his belief throughout his earthly life and guaranteed of eternal life. However, Jesus said that many would profess belief and delude others that they were true Christians when they didn't have a true conversion, and thus would fall away when the going gets rough, and possibly even to the point of specifically repudiating that belief openly before God and man. Also, there are also some examples of people who have professed belief but hid some specific unbelief or doubt and paid with their lives for that lie. Becoming a believer requires an honest confession of, and full acknowledgement of guilt for one's previous sins, and acceptance of a new life in Christ. This does not mean that one would automatically stop sinning, but that a true believer would recognize the error of what one was doing and desire earnestly not to do wrong. Jesus promised that both the before-acceptance and after-acceptance sins would be "...washed white as snow."

Also, there are examples in several of Paul's letters and in the book of James that lay out how a true believer will think and approach life once he has fully accepted Christ and Holy Spirit is in his heart.

<u>An eleventh theme is that Christ will return</u> in power to judge and bring peace to the world and to all people who are called by his name. And that this coming will be like a thief in the night, and no man can know when it will happen. So believers must always be ready for his coming. But trying to predict the exact date of his coming is a futile exercise and can have dire consequences.

In summary, this Jesus was such a powerful influence during a ministry of only 3 years that he changed the world, and the Bible gives a clear picture of how this has happened. Thus, both his life and the Bible are remarkable and enduring.

THE BIBLE - AFTER THE EARTHLY MINISTRY OF CHRIST

All of what appears in the New Testament took place during a period of about 90 years, but it has profoundly affected history for the next 2000 years. All of the books of the New Testament were written between about 45 AD and 90 AD. They were preserved as separate books until about 325 AD when they were combined by a group of believing scholars into the document that we know today. A few years after Christ was crucified, the Jewish Zealots lead a rebellion against Roman rule, which resulted in the final destruction of the Jewish temple in Jerusalem and the killing of the last Zealots at Masada (a hilltop fortress south of Jerusalem) in about 70 AD. But the number of Christians grew remarkably in the Roman Empire, and Roman emperors started considering Christianity a threat to their rule. They began a campaign to eliminate it, making a spectacle of killing Christians in the coliseum in Rome, and culminating in Nero's attempt to convince people that the Christians had caused the burning of Rome. (Historians say that he actually had the fire set himself to make way for a new palace.) However, Christianity continued to flourish. At the same time, the Roman Empire began to decline. Rome itself was racked by riots resulting from the population getting used to government food handouts and the government becoming too poor to give them. The Roman army, so fierce in previous generations, became corrupt and lazy. Then Rome was invaded by Vandals, Goths, and Huns from variously Africa, Eastern Europe and Russia. The leaders of the Empire decided to move the whole government to the new city of Constantinople on the waterway connecting the Black Sea and the Mediterranean Sea. It was named after the Roman Emperor Constantine. Constantine became a Christian, and in about 325 AD authorized the assembly of the various Jewish and Christian writings into a single document to be called the Judeo/Christian Bible.

The group who put the Bible together also accepted the Old Testament as assembled by Jewish scholars between 200 BC and 50 AD, but rejected several books called the Apocrypha as not inspired or authentic. They also rejected several candidate writings proposed for the New Testament as also not proved to be inspired or authentic. Thus, the Bible took the current form and content about 1700 years ago and has had no basic changes since..

A few years later, Jerome, a Roman scholar, was commissioned to translate the Bible from its original Hebrew, Greek, and Aramaic languages into Vulgate, the basically Latin language of the common people of the Roman Empire, so that everyone could read and understand it. (Education was encouraged in the Roman Empire so that the majority of Romans could read and write.) Christianity began to spread exponentially throughout the know world. Strong Christian centers of worship were established in Egypt and eastern Africa as far south as Ethiopia. It spread to Persia and Spain, and even as far north and west to Ireland. Even the Vandals, a violent barbarian people of North Africa were converted to Christianity.

But, after the fall of the Roman Empire and the advent of subsequent "Dark Ages", the people of Europe were no longer taught to read, and the Vulgate (Latin) language died except among the remnant of church leaders and monks in isolated monasteries. Also, during the same period, about 600 AD the Muslim faith came into existence. Many in the mid-east became adherents. Unfortunately, Mohamed, its originator was a warlord by culture, and even though he taught peace, many to his teachings were tainted by his strong ideals that people not of his faith should be converted or eliminated. Some of the more violent adherents of the Muslim faith began to wipe out Jewish and Christian believers and the churches in Judea, Lebanon, and Turkey. And they established a center of Muslim worship in Jerusalem.

By the 6th century, a center of Christian church leadership had been reestablished in Rome and became known as the Roman Catholic Church. Unfortunately, one of the things the church leaders there decided was that the Bible was too much of a mystery to be understood by the common people, and held all church services in Latin, which almost no-one could any longer understand. Thus, the services (called Masses) became more ritual than Biblical teaching. The Roman Catholic Church also established itself and a political power, appointing various kings over time as "Holy Roman Emperors", who built armies and fought bitter and bloody wars with each other, even between some Christian governments and religious movements over both territory and religious differences. And the church itself became corrupt, becoming rich on taxes and sales of blessings and dispensations.

It is interesting to note that even the best of men and nations, once they have become powerful have a tendency to revert to the savage practices of the pre-Christian era, and to forget the whole of the ideals of the teachings of Christ. The savagery and brutality of these powerful, so-called Christian movements have even often exceeded those of Babylon and other ancient cultures.

In about 900 AD, mostly illiterate and uneducated Europeans, lead by ardent church leaders, began to organize "Crusades" to take back the "Holy Land" from the Muslims and restore Jerusalem as a Christian capitol. Not only did the crusades fail but they fomented a massive retaliation by Muslim forces, who, over the next 200 years, virtually wiped out Christianity in the Middle East and built a Muslim holy temple (the Dome of The Rock) where the Jewish temple once stood. They also invaded Europe, conquering Spain and parts of southeastern Europe, getting as far as Vienna, Austria. They overran Constantinople, changing its name to Istanbul. It is now in part of Muslim Turkey. There are still a relatively small number of Christian groups remaining in Turkey and other parts of the Middle East. But they have had little influence on history since that period. The largest of these is the Eastern (or Greek) Orthodox Church.

In the 1400s, Christian forces in Europe recaptured Spain and drove out the Muslims. But they were immediately followed by ardent Catholic church leaders, who set up the "inquisition" to torture and execute anyone who they even suspected of being non-Catholics. They practically wiped out the Jewish population of Spain. They also carried the faith to the Americas and forcefully converted or killed many Native Americans in Mexico and Central and South America.

Then, also in the 1400s, kings and church leaders in northern Europe began to chafe under the Roman Catholic Church domination. Martin Luther, a leader of the Catholic Church in Germany, became disenchanted with the church corruption, and broke away, setting up the Lutheran Church. At about the same time English leaders did the same in England and created the Church of England. In the 1500s and 1600s, Christians decided also to break away from the limitations of using the Latin language in the church services and to again translate the Bible into the language of the people. The first couple of people who translated the Bible into English were executed (burned at the stake) as heretics (by those who had reverted to savagery). However, a printer, Guttenberg, in Germany, translated the Bible into the German language and mass printed it for everyday use. Then, King James, the King of England, decreed that an official version be created in English by Christian scholars. They did an amazing job, and the King James Version of the Bible became the translation used in most non-Catholic, English speaking churches for several hundred years. Even after this, there were several brutal wars between Christian factions in England and Ireland that resulted in mass torture and death. But as the British Empire grew and spread around the world, so did the King James Bible. In fact, it began being used as a text book for teaching both the English language and Christianity in almost every corner of the earth, (except the Middle East, which was still dominated by the Muslims, who have made it illegal to do so).

The framers of the US Declaration of Independence and the US Constitution in the 1700s drew heavily on Bible teachings and contemporary writings of strong Christian philosophers in creating those documents. The Ten Commandments have almost always been recognized as the foundation of US law. Interestingly, the French revolutionaries tried to copy the US revolutionary model when leading the French revolution against the tyranny and excesses of the French King. They promoted humanitarian ideals, but unlike in the creation of the new America, they left God and the Bible out of the equation. This led to a 15 year reign of terror, with many executions, which only ended when another king, Napoleon Bonaparte came into power. And even Napoleon became a tyrant, leading a great war that resulted in much destruction and many deaths.

Then, in the 19th century in Eastern Europe and Russia, there grew up a corrupted, unreasoned attack on the people of Jewish heritage, which resulted in heavy persecution and many murders. This movement was generally referred to as the "pogroms". It forced many of those of Jewish heritage to migrate to other parts of the world and others to move to ghettos with poor living conditions. The root excuse for the pogroms was to reek continued punishment on them for killing Christ, even though the perpetrators were often not Christians themselves and probably had not read or understood the Bible messages. Then in the 20th century this was made even worse by Adolph Hitler who literally ordered property confiscation and murder of millions, in order to, in his twisted ideas, purge the world of the race of people who "killed Christ". And to replace them, he promoted idea of genetically producing a "master race" of humans he felt would be more suited to rule and to be more like little gods on earth. He called them Arians. Unfortunately, Hitler and his minions seem to have not noticed that Abraham, the progenitor of the Jewish people, was identified in Genesis as a member of a people group called "Arameans" (Arian for short?). Also, unreasoned hatred is an ultimate evil, and seems work its deadliest when an easily defined target can be identified. The Bible, and especially the New Testament teaches love and forgiveness, but if this Biblical message is not read or understood, it cannot work for good.

In the 20th Century, Christian scholars realized that the English language was drifting away from the language used in King James' time, and decided to update the King James Bible to get rid of its archaic language (i.e. the word "debt" being no longer synonymous with "transgression" and the frequent use of the archaic words "thee" and "thou"). They even went back to recently discovered texts that were even older than the ones available to the King James translators. Unfortunately, in doing so, the floodgates were opened, and a number of competing translations were published. The one most commonly used today in non-catholic churches is the New International Version (NIV). However, there are strong adherents to other 20th century translations, and some still prefer the King James translation. The Catholic Church has also begun publishing an official English language translation (called the N.A.B. Bible) and has started holding many masses (Catholic church services) in English.

A couple of the recent translations have tried to deny the virgin birth of Jesus, have tried to change the Bible to make it gender neutral (eliminate references to the differences between man and woman), or have tried to delete the parts of the Bible that condemn homosexuality. However, none of these are true translations, but are modifications of the original text to suit beliefs of special interest individuals or groups. Some really evil people have tried to use out-of-context pieces or corruptions of the Bible to do great damage to culture and society. The ideas of witches, demon possession, and Devil worship are some of these. Other people have tried to predict the future using specific out-of-context Biblical texts with sometimes disastrous results, such as the Jonestown massacre. .

Important things to remember about the Bible though, are (1) to understand the Bible, it needs to be taken as a whole, not just as individually inspiring, or dissimilar, or sometimes apparently conflicting parts, (2) to recognize how its teachings fit specific cultures and periods of human existence, (3) to recognize the consistency of its texts over the period of at least 2000 years of human history during the time in which it was written, (4) to see its proclamation of not only the brotherhood of mankind but also the powerful declaration of the supremacy, justice, mercy, and inerrancy of the creator of the universe, (5) to recognize that the Bible offers believers a way to ultimate inner peace on earth and eternal life afterwards, and (6) to realize that most of the translators of the Bible have tried to keep it as pure as possible to the original Hebrew/Greek/Latin Bible that was put together over 1700 years ago, and parts of which were written down at least 4000 years ago that in some cases were verbal lore long before that. Thus, it is the oldest and longest lasting book of continuous history and religion ever published, telling the story of all of existence, space, time, and man.

And today, the Judeo/Christian Bible is the most often purchased and most widely circulated of any book in history, and even in this supposedly post Christian era is still every year at the top of the best sellers list. It must be noted that the laws of most civilized countries in the world are structured around the concepts of the Ten Commandments. And every part of the Bible is still very useful as a book of faith, hope, love, and wisdom and as a guide to conscience and law-and-order for a civilized world. Its sayings and passages are most often quoted of any book. **It is truly a miracle.**

POSTSCRIPT

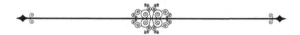

*   If, upon conclusion of the reading of this document, a person is lead to a desire for more in-depth study of the messages of the Bible, or further, to a belief in the truths expressed in it, **this is the primary hoped-for result of this book.**

*   If it leads a person to a belief that there is a meaning to life that is beyond the mundane, this is a desired benefit for the reader.

*   If it leads a person to a desire to live a better life, this is a benefit to both the reader and those whom that person comes in contact.

*   If it leads a person to a belief that the Bible is a true and real word of God, the Creator of the Universe, spoken to mankind, this is an inspiration.

*   If it leads a person to the conviction that the Jesus of the New Testament is the Christ, the promised one of the Old Testament, this is a great outcome.

* If it leads a person to the belief that Jesus Christ was sent by God to be the savior of the world, and to offer eternal life to mankind, this makes this document worthwhile.

* If it leads a person toward a desire for the acceptance of Jesus Christ into one's own heart as personal savior, that person should go for it and not look back.

Printed in the United States
By Bookmasters